DOYLE BRUNSON

MY 50 MOST
MEMORABLE HANDS

DOYLE BRUNSON

••••••••••••••••••••••••••••••••

MY 50 MOST
MEMORABLE HANDS

CARDOZA PUBLISHING

Cardoza Publishing is the foremost gaming publisher in the world, with a library of over 200 up-to-date and easy-to-read books and strategies. These authoritative works are written by the top experts in their fields and with more than 9,000,000 books in print, represent the best-selling and most popular gaming books anywhere.

FIRST EDITION

Copyright © 2007 by Doyle Brunson
- All Rights Reserved -

Library of Congress Catalog Card No: 2006940637
ISBN: 1-58042-202-0

Cover and Interior Design by Sara Cardoza

Visit our web site—www.cardozapub.com—or write for a full list of books and computer strategies.

CARDOZA PUBLISHING
P.O. Box 1500, Cooper Station, New York, NY 10276
Phone (800) 577-WINS
email: cardozapub@aol.com
www.cardozapub.com

This book is dedicated to all the players I have played with the last 50 years.

TABLE OF CONTENTS

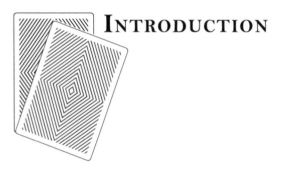# INTRODUCTION

I've played millions of hands since I turned pro fifty years ago. I was blessed to have a great memory. I can still remember the names of basketball players I played against and can remember how many points I scored when I played them. It's nothing I have done; it's just a gift.

The hands that I detail in this book are in no particular order of importance, just the ones that come to mind first. As we grow older we live a lot in our memories. I feel very fortunate to still be playing poker and creating even more memories. I hope you enjoy some of mine—and profit from them.

 # MEMORABLE HAND #1

This is easily the most memorable hand in my poker career. I had been playing in the local games in Ft. Worth, Texas since turning pro in 1957. I had developed my skills, playing night and day on Exchange Avenue, the toughest place I have ever been. I had been winning consistently for several months and I felt it was time to try my hand on the "Texas Circuit," which consisted of thirty or forty towns around Texas where poker games were held regularly. The Circuit had a nucleus of professional poker players who determined where the poker games would be held.

I was only twenty-four years old and nobody outside of Fort Worth knew anything about my ability as a poker player. So, when I started playing on The Circuit, even though I won much more than I lost, I hadn't received any real respect from the touring pros. Then one rainy night in Brenham, Texas, after a three day marathon poker game, this hand came up.

MY HAND	**JOHNNY MOSS**	**CARLO**

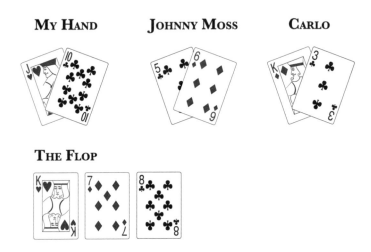

THE FLOP

Carlo was first to act in this unraised pot. The blinds were $100/$200. Carlo bet $380. Johnny Moss called and I called. The fourth card was the deuce of spades. The board looked like this:

THE TURN

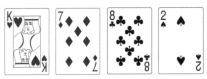

Everyone checked including me. The fifth card was the 3♦.

THE RIVER

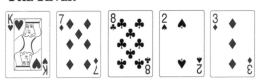

Carlo checked and Moss bet $4,000. I thought this bet was very unusual because it looked like he was trying to push us out of the pot. I was sure he had drawn at some kind of a straight, and I had drawn at the highest possible straight, so I had to have him beat.

So, I called Moss with jack-high! I correctly figured Carlo couldn't overcall. I won that pot and was considered a world-class player by my peers from that point on. I've always remembered that hand!

# MEMORABLE
HAND #2

This hand is especially memorable because of the violent ending. This occurred in my first year of playing poker professionally. I was on Exchange Avenue where shootings, knife fights, and fistfights happened every day and were actually expected. We were playing in the back of Exchange Avenue Pool Hall, which had illegal gambling in the back room. There was a crap game and two poker games going one weekend night. I remember we were playing in a 50¢ ante, $2/$4 blind game, half ace-to-five lowball and half five-card draw high.

Around midnight a distraught husband walked into the back room and calmly pulled a pistol, put it up to one of the poker player's heads and shot him.

The shooter turned and left the room.

All the gamblers in the room where the shooting took place ran out the back doors because we didn't want to be questioned by the police. There was a small creek running behind the pool hall and we ran through it. I still remember how cold that small creek was.

I was in the middle of a draw high pot and had just bet

$20 with my hand when the shooting happened. My hand was: A♠ A♦ 7♣ 7♦ 2♦. I have always called this hand "next to the dead man's hand," referencing Wild Bill Hitchcock's famous aces and eights dead man's hand.

Next to the Dead Man's Hand

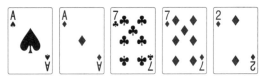

Most arguments were over women or drugs. I think this was over a woman. I still have dreams of this incident, the man's brains splattered over the wall behind the poker game. I never heard of anyone being arrested for the shooting. The police didn't investigate killings very much on Exchange Avenue.

MEMORABLE HAND #3

In 1976 at the World Series of Poker, I played a pot with Jesse Alto, a professional poker player from Corpus Christi, Texas. It's probably the best-known hand ever played and will go down in poker history. Jesse and I were the final two players in the championship event that had lasted three days. I had about three-fourths of the chips and had just won a big pot from Jesse, who was a notorious steamer. I knew if I could beat him another pot right away, it would be over and the championship would be mine.

Sure enough, he raised the next pot. My hand was the 10♠ 2♠. Ordinarily I wouldn't play this hand, but in this situation I called. The flop was A♥ J♠ 10♥.

DOYLE   **JESSE**

THE FLOP

Jesse bet with the top two pair and I called because I knew he could have any two cards and I had a pair and a backdoor flush. The next card was the 2♣, giving me two pair. He bet, I moved in on him, and he called. The fifth card, or river card, was the 10♦ giving me a full house and the WSOP Championship.

1976 WSOP Final Championship Hand

DOYLE   JESSE ALTO

THE BOARD

That is a perfect example of situational poker. A hand that I would almost never play became the "Doyle Brunson" hand. That was the first of the two 10-2 hands that immortalized those cards.

I'll discuss the second part of the 10-2 saga later in this book.

MEMORABLE HAND #4

I've only made two significant royal flushes in my career and ironically, they were against the same player, Bobby Baldwin. Bobby, who later went on to be the best known gaming executive in the world (CEO of Mirage Corporations, former president of the Bellagio), was one of the young, great players in the early 1980s. I was fortunate enough to beat really big hands with my two royals and I obviously remember these hands with great pleasure.

I have included both of these hands together because it would be hard to separate them. It was at the Golden Nugget in 1981 and I had raised the pot with Q♠ 10♠. Bobby had two jacks and had called.

DOYLE   **BOBBY**

THE FLOP

Bobby was a great player and he played this hand beautifully. He was first to act and he bet right out, thinking this flop could have easily helped me. I raised him, hoping he wasn't on a strong hand, but he called me. The fourth card was the 4♦ and Bobby checked and I checked behind him. The river was the ace of spaces, giving me the royal flush. Bobby bet, I moved in, and of course he called. The pot was almost $200,000, which was a huge pot in the 1980s.

DOYLE   **BOBBY**

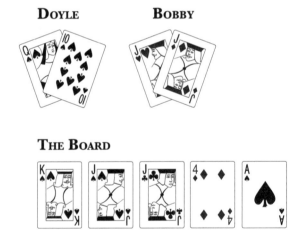

THE BOARD

In 1993, we were at the Bicycle Club in Los Angeles playing $3,000/$6,000 limit hold'em. In a raised pot, I held the J♦ 10♦ and Bobby held two black aces. The flop was A♦ K♦ 4♥.

DOYLE   BOBBY

THE FLOP

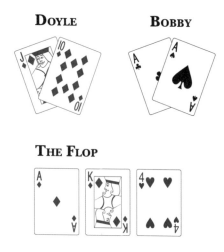

Bobby bet. I raised and he reraised. I called and the turn was the Q♦, giving me a royal flush. Bobby bet. I raised and he called. The river was the 4♣ giving Bobby aces full.

DOYLE   BOBBY

THE BOARD

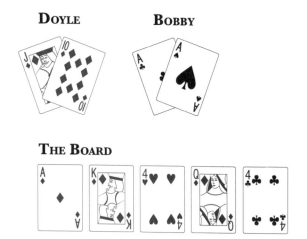

After three bets and raises, Bobby made the most unbelievable laydown I have ever seen. He told me later he thought I had to have the royal flush to make the last raise. Even so, I think he should have called. To this day, I tell him I had kings full.

MEMORABLE HAND #5

In the early 1970s, hold'em was just beginning to catch on in Las Vegas. I had just moved to Vegas from Texas and was trying to promote hold'em because the local pros hadn't played this game much and weren't very good. Johnny Moss had also moved to Vegas and was running the card room at the Aladdin Hotel and Casino.

I walked into the card room one day and couldn't believe my eyes. There was a six-handed hold'em game going on with stacks of chips and money in front of some of the biggest high rollers in town. This game lasted for forty-five days. All the hold'em players in the South had heard about the game and were flocking to Vegas to play.

Included in this group was my friend and longtime opponent, Crandell Addington. Crandell was one of the original "Texas Rounders" and was a great player. I knew his aggressive style would be a force to be reckoned with. I decided to fight fire with fire and play extremely fast against him.

After several days of play, Crandell and I were the two big winners and we had all our money on the table when this hand came up. I had two sevens and Crandell had two kings. He raised and I called. The flop was K♣ 4♥ 2♦.

DOYLE   **CRANDELL**

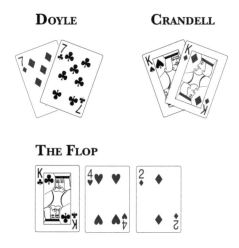

THE FLOP

Crandell bet and I raised him, hoping to push him out of the pot. He only called hoping to beat me in a big pot. The fourth card was a 7, giving me a set of sevens. Crandell bet again. I raised him, confidently believing my three sevens were good. Crandell called and the river was the last 7.

DOYLE   **CRANDELL**

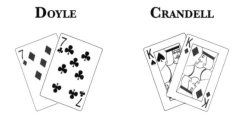

THE BOARD

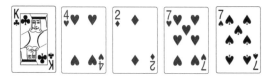

Crandell checked, I bet, and he moved in. I had the nuts, so I called and sent my toughest opponent back to Texas. There was almost a million dollars in that pot and the old timers told me it was the biggest pot in Vegas history at that point.

MEMORABLE HAND #6

I have to rank the hand that won my second World Championship very high in my book. It was in 1977 in the main event. I became the chip leader early in the first day and never relinquished that top spot. I was at the absolute peak of my game, and this was one of the few times the first day leader won the tournament. I had made all the right decisions and had 80 percent of the chips when it got down to the final two players.

Bones Berland was my opponent. He was a promising young pro who had a rare blood disorder and died a few years after this tournament. We were sparring around when this hand came up. I had a 10-2 offsuit and Bones had 8-5. I was in the big blind and nobody raised. The flop was 10♦ 8♠ 5♥.

DOYLE   **BONES**

THE FLOP

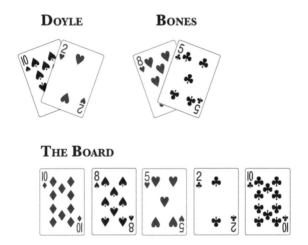

I checked. Bones, trying to trap me, also checked his two pair. The fourth card was the 2♣, giving me the bigger two pair hand. I bet and Bones moved in on me. I called and the fifth card was another 10 making my full house, tens over twos, the winning hand two years in a row.

1977 WSOP Final Championship Hand

DOYLE   BONES

THE BOARD

So now the 10-2 became the "Doyle Brunson" for all time and the most famous hand in poker. I never liked my nickname, "Texas Dolly," nor do I especially like the 10-2 being my official hand, but there isn't anything I can do about it.

What most people don't know is that the 10-2 almost won

a third WSOP Championship in 1981. Perry Green had the 10-2 of clubs and had Stu Unger all in. Perry had an open-end straight draw and a flush draw but missed his hand. Had he made it, the 10-2 would be even more famous.

 # Memorable Hand #7

When I was playing the Texas Circuit, one of the better games was in San Antonio, Texas. It was by invitation only because of the large numbers of businessmen that played poker here. I was one of the Texas rounders that the non-pros loved to play against because I gave a lot of action in any poker game I played in. So I always got invited when there was a seat available.

This was a game in the early 1960s. We were playing $40/$80/$160 limit hold'em, which was considered to be a high limit game in those days. It meant you could raise $40 before the flop, $80 on the flop, and $160 on the fourth and fifth cards. It was structured that way to create action, and it did just that!

There were eight players in this game, among them a very good professional poker player named Gilbert Hess and an amateur player named Guy Aldridge.

I had two aces and had raised before the flop with Gilbert and Guy both calling. The flop came A♦ 4♣ 2♥.

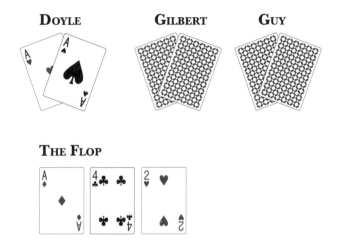

DOYLE **GILBERT** **GUY**

THE FLOP

I bet. Gilbert raised, Guy raised and I capped the betting at four bets. The fourth card was another deuce and we capped the betting again with four bets. The fifth card was a 4.

The board looked like this:

THE BOARD

I had strongly suspected Gilbert had flopped a set so I checked. Gilbert bet, Guy raised, and I folded aces full. Everyone praised me for making a great play but in reality it was pretty obvious one or both of them had quads. Sure enough, Gilbert had four deuces and Guy had four 4s.

The operator of that game was Tom Moore who later went to Reno and opened the Holiday Casino. That was where the first poker tournament was held and was called the Texas Gamblers Convention. Jack Binion and his father, Benny

Binion, came to Reno for the event, and when Tom retired back to Texas, they moved the tournament to the Horseshoe Casino in Las Vegas.

This event is now known as the World Series of Poker.

MEMORABLE
HAND #8

There were many great professional poker players when I started playing regularly on the Texas Circuit. There was James Roy, Aubrey Day, Pat Renfro, Doc Ramsey, and many more. But, the one player I kept hearing about was Johnny Moss.

I asked, "What's so special about him?" Finally, when I was twenty-five years old, I was playing in a good no-limit hold'em game in Houston, Texas, when Johnny came in and sat down. I was playing well and I was very confident so I welcomed the chance to play against the man everyone said was the best. I was also sure that he had heard of me because everyone was always saying I was a young Johnny Moss.

So, there was tension in the air every time Johnny and I played a pot. I had been very lucky all night and had won several big pots from Johnny. Johnny was a big loser when this hand came up. I had the K♦ and 9♦. Johnny had K♣ 2♣. The flop was K♠ 9♥ 2♦.

DOYLE   **JOHNNY**

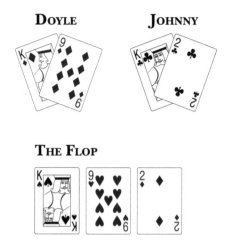

THE FLOP

I bet. Johnny raised and I reraised. Johnny showed me his hand and threw it away. Pretty impressive laydown! I told him I had A-K after I threw my hand in but I could tell he didn't believe me.

I repeatedly beat Johnny every big pot the rest of the night. I observed how he handled the adversity and kept his cool, making the correct judgment on most every hand. I was a $150,000 winner, most of it coming from pots against Johnny. He was still even at the end of the night and I knew why he was considered to be "the man" in the poker world.

If I ever had a mentor, it was Johnny Moss.

MEMORABLE HAND #9

In the early 1980s, Eric Drache and I opened a card room at the old Silverbird on the Las Vegas strip. We were in direct competition with the Dunes Card Room for the high limit games. I knew all the high rollers from the South and I invited them to come and play at our room, all expenses paid. They came in droves and we had some of the greatest high limit poker games the world has ever seen.

Major Riddle, the owner of the Silverbird, was a terrible poker player; but he loved the game. He lost millions in our card room and all the players came to play with him. Also, I had known Jimmy Chagra, the convicted drug dealer from El Paso, Texas. Jimmy came out to play and astounded all of us with his total disregard for money. He was betting $100,000 a hand in the 21 games and shooting craps sky high. I saw him tip a cocktail waitress $10,000 for bringing him a Coca-Cola. But his first love in gambling was poker, and we had huge games with Jimmy losing bales of cash.

We were playing deuce-to-seven no-limit lowball with Jimmy when one of the strangest plays I've ever seen happened.

We were anteing $500 with $3,000/$6,000 blinds. That would be a big game by today's standards, but back then there were life-changing decisions being made every day. Jimmy opened the pot for $20,000 and I had this hand:

DOYLE

I raised $60,000 and Jimmy reraised me $220,000. He had $42,000 left, so I just called him hoping I could keep him from drawing. To my surprise, Jimmy threw two cards away. I must have felt badly for him making such a terrible play, because I said: "Do you want to save the money you have left?"

Jimmy laughed and said: "Oh, no, you aren't getting away with that." And, he bet the $42,000 before he looked at the cards he drew. Naturally I called as I was probably a 10-1 favorite to win this hand. Jimmy caught two face cards, smiled, and quit the game.

I guess if you live long enough, you'll see everything.

MEMORABLE
HAND #10

In the early days of my career on Exchange Avenue in Ft. Worth, Texas, there was a poker game in every pool hall, beer joint, and even the hotels. Exchange Avenue had to be an enigma, a throwback to the old west. All the cowboys, truck drivers, pimps, thieves, and numerous other unsavory characters kept the poker games going full blast night and day. These were some of the hardest living, rowdiest, and most colorful men that the world has ever known. I got to know most of them because of my passion for poker.

I played almost every waking hour. It was here that I played my longest session, five days and five nights without sleeping. I only stopped to eat and go to the bathroom. I didn't do drugs but drank tons of coffee to stay awake.

After the fourth day of play with several of the same players that started the game, we were playing ace-to-five no-limit lowball. An employee of the local slaughterhouse named Virgil had been playing as long as I had. The difference was he was taking pills to stay awake. Also, he was drinking heavily and smoking one cigarette after another.

I had known Virgil for a year or so and I had cautioned him about taking drugs and drinking at the same time. He and I got into a pot and this was my hand:

DOYLE

I brought the pot in. Virgil raised and I called. I threw the king away, drew one card and caught a 7. I bet, Virgil raised all his money and I called. I said "Seven," and turned my hand over. Virgil looked and then said: "I don't have a five in mine" and turned over A-2-3-4-7.

DOYLE

VIRGIL

I said, "That's good." He took a drink of Old Charter Whisky, reached for the pot, and dropped dead right on the spot.

That is when I found out how cold-blooded poker players can be. All of us had known Virgil and had played with him many times. After the paramedics took him away the game resumed, and we played another twenty-four hours.

MEMORABLE
HAND #11

In poker tournaments, one of the prime times to increase your chips is right before the final table. When there are only nine places at the final table and there are ten to fifteen players left, it is amazing how tight the remaining players get. Years ago, the tournaments only paid the final table, as opposed to today's tournaments when the payouts go much higher. So, because I always play to win the tournament instead of just getting into the money, I always played liberally when crunch time came.

When we were down to ten players in the 1986 WSOP, I was hammering away at the pots, building my chips up, when Jay Heimowitz and I played a big pot. Jay was an amateur from New York but had been playing at the highest levels for years, and I had a lot of respect for his game.

Jay brought it in from the first position, which is a very dangerous thing because I knew Jay had a good hand. I looked and I had two kings so I made an unusually large raise. I was thinking Jay would pass unless he had two aces, A-K or perhaps A-Q. I really felt he would pass any other hand, even two queens. If he had reraised me, I would have given him credit for two aces and thrown my hand away. To my surprise, he called! The flop was Q♥ 10♦ 2♣.

DOYLE　　　　**JAY**

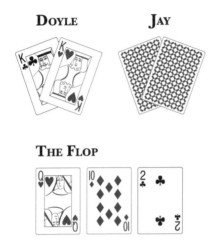

THE FLOP

I knew Jay wanted to be at that final table. I didn't want him to make a straight if he had A-K, and I had A-Q beat, so I moved all my chips in. To my astonishment, he called.

I said, "Did you have to do that?"

He said, "I've got you beat."

And he turned over a Q-10 offsuit. I caught an ace and a jack to make a straight and eliminated him.

DOYLE　　　　**JAY**

THE BOARD

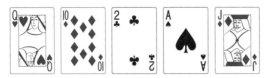

I asked him later why he had played such a poor hand at that point in the tournament. He said, "I didn't want the other players to see you push me around when I opened from the #1 hole."

Jay now has a total of five bracelets from the WSOP and is still playing great poker in his 60s.

MEMORABLE HAND #12

In the 2004 WSOP there were an astounding 2,576 players, quite a far cry from the first event when just six of us sat down. The mega explosion of poker has been attributed to TV exposure and Internet poker and I believe that the tournaments are going to get bigger and bigger. It's not only the WSOP that's growing in popularity, but also the World Poker Tour and all the different tournaments that are springing up all over the world.

I had played well in the 2004 series and had outlasted over 2,600 players. It was down to 53 players when a weird pot came up. I was in the #8 seat and the #1 seat had the button. Everyone passed to me.

I looked and had:

DOYLE

I said, "All in," which meant I bet all my chips, almost $400,000. There was about $60,000 in antes and blinds in the pot and I wanted to win it without a contest. The #1 seat passed and the #2 seat, who was Bradley Berman, said, "I'm going to raise it."

The dealer said, "Doyle is already all in."

Bradley said, "Oh, I didn't hear him. I'm out."

The dealer called the supervisor over and told him Bradley didn't hear me say "all in" because of a commotion at the table next to us. The supervisor sympathetically said the rule is when someone says "raise," they have to bet more than the raise if they have enough chips to do so. That meant Brad had to put my $400,000 raise into the pot plus his remaining $250,000. The big blind passed. So it was just us two, heads-up, for all my chips.

Brad had an A-7 offsuit, a hand he wouldn't even consider playing against me.

The flop was:

THE FLOP

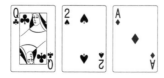

The turn and river didn't help me, and I was out of the tournament on a fluke. But, rules are rules and I understood. As I got up to leave, the entire room stood and applauded as I exited.

It was a touching moment I will never forget.

MEMORABLE
HAND #13

Back in the late 1950s our main game was hold'em, but we played a lot of deuce-to-seven no-limit lowball. There were more bad lowball players than there were hold'em players so I welcomed the chance to play it. One of the best deuce-to-seven players was Freddie (Sarge) Ferris. Sarge, as we all called him, was the most fearless player I have ever faced. He was a legend back in the South when I first started playing on the Texas Circuit. The Texas Circuit included all the neighboring states of Texas. That included Louisiana, where I first met Sarge.

I was twenty-four or twenty-five years old at the time and was virtually unknown in the gambling world. I didn't have much money, $10,000 or so, and I had it all on the table in Shreveport, Louisiana, playing two-to-seven lowball with a group of traveling pros and two or three local businessmen. I was in awe of the players in the game I had been hearing about for years. There was Sarge, Johnny Moss, Aubrey Day from Alabama, and Broomcorn—yes the same Broomcorn I wrote about in *Super System 1* and *Super System 2*.

We had been playing for two or three hours. I remember I

was a $4,000 winner when this pot came up. I brought it in for $1,500. Broomcorn called and Moss moved in $20,000 more. I thought he was just trying to muscle us out of the pot so I called with the rest of my money. Then Broomcorn called.

My hand was:

DOYLE

I threw away a 3 and Broomcorn and Moss both threw a card away. Moss said to me, "If one of us wins this pot big boy, let's split it."

That confirmed my suspicion that Moss didn't have a very good hand. Obviously, I had the best draw possible so even though I had no more money I said, "No, thanks."

I caught a king and Broomcorn won the pot, making a 9-8. Johnny Moss had been drawing at a 9 so I had the better hand by far. But I lost, and as I was getting up to quit, Sarge called me aside and said to me, "I like the way you gamble. I have $100,000 on deposit here. Use all of it or any part of it. Pay me back when you can."

That started a friendship that lasted 40 years until Sarge died. Many years later Sarge loaned me $800,000 when I got broke betting football. I paid him back the same year. I will never forget him.

MEMORABLE HAND #14

The Eagle's Club, a fraternal organization in Odessa, Texas, was one of the regular stops on the Texas Circuit. Sailor Roberts, Amarillo Slim Preston, and I were traveling together using the same bankroll to play out of. We became partners for several reasons:

a. To have someone to drive to the games with.

b. To have protection against hijackers and robbers.

c. To have enough money to play in the larger games.

While playing as a team worked to our disadvantage because everybody knew we did it, we liked the camaraderie between us.

We stopped in Odessa after driving over 500 miles because we had heard about the high stakes games they were having at the Eagle's Club. The main attraction was a retail liquor store owner named "Pinky" Rhoden. Pinky had stores all across Texas and was a very wealthy man who enjoyed poker. The problem was that Pinky always quit when he got a few thousand dollars ahead. My mission was to get him loser where he would play for a longer period of time.

After a few hours of playing, Pinky was about even and I had tripled my $10,000 buy in. Pinky used what he called a "master chip," which meant he was calling all bets. I picked up the A♣ 4♣ and Pinky had two red kings. Pinky raised and I called. The flop came K♣ 3♦ 5♣.

Doyle   **Pinky**

The Flop

After I had raised Pinky's first bet, he threw in the master chip declaring, "I'm tapping you." This meant that if I wanted to call, I had to put in about $27,000 in addition to the $3,000 I had already had in there.

I was pretty sure he had three kings, but I saw a chance to get Pinky loser and have a good game. Pinky turned his three kings up after I called him and asked if I had a set (three of a kind).

I said, "No, I'm drawing."

He went berserk, wanting to know how I could call that money without as much as a pair. Pinky demanded to cut the cards and when I didn't object he reached over and cut the cards. The dealer dealt the 7♥ and the 9♣, completing my flush.

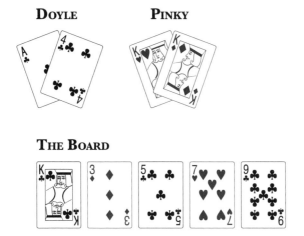

DOYLE   **PINKY**

THE BOARD

Ordinarily I wouldn't have called a bet like that, but my objective had been reached. Pinky was loser and the game went for a week with Pinky losing well over a million dollars. Between me and Amarillo Slim, we won almost half of the money.

Sometimes you have to gamble to maximize your profits.

MEMORABLE
HAND #15

In the late 1950s I graduated from the stockyard games in Ft. Worth, Texas, to the bigger games in downtown Ft. Worth. We played at the Diane Hotel where the Convention Center site is today. While we had our share of low-caliber people playing there, lots of local, respectable businessmen played there also.

This is where I met Bryan (Sailor) Roberts, an ex-football star from San Angelo, Texas. Sailor was easily the best player in the game and I watched every move he made very closely. Sailor gave the illusion of being a very liberal, loose player when, in fact, he was a very tight, cautious player. We were playing deuce-to-seven no-limit lowball when a large pot came up between us. I remember I had my rent money on the table—which wasn't that unusual—and had it all in the pot.

My hand was:

DOYLE

Sailor acted first and stood pat, meaning he drew no cards. After careful consideration, my reasoning told me I should throw the 8 away and draw one. While it was possible Sailor had a 9-6 or 9-5, there were more hands he could have that would beat mine. I correctly thought he was at least a 3-1 favorite to beat my hand. I determined this from the long hours I had watched him. I caught a 3 to beat Sailor's 8-6 and won the pot.

DOYLE

After the game was over, Sailor took me to breakfast and we discussed that hand and my reasoning behind it. He complimented me on my play and became one of my all-time best friends. The sad part of this story is he somehow got hooked on drugs when he was fifty-eight years old and died.

I think he could have been one of the all-time great poker players if he could have applied himself to the game.

MEMORABLE
HAND #16

I was a no-limit player my entire life until I moved to Las Vegas in 1969. After seven years of playing only no-limit games there, I decided I had to branch out and learn the limit games. It is important for today's players—even more than back then—to learn all forms of poker. Most of the games are limit and there is lots of money to be won.

I can remember starting out playing high-low split no-declare at the Flamingo in 1975. Johnny Moss, Puggy Pearson, Nick Vachicano, Jimmy Cassela, and I were playing and nobody, including me, was playing very well. I had played enough in college to know the concept of playing for the low side of the pot and letting the high fall where it would. A young, baby-faced, blond-headed kid was watching us play; and then he sat down in our $400/$800 eight-handed high-low game.

That was my first look at David "Chip" Reese. He sat down with his entire bankroll of $8,000. Chip had just graduated from Dartmouth and was on his way to law school at Stanford when he stopped in Vegas. He had been there for a month playing in the $5/$10 and $10/$20 stud games. Chip had built his $400 bankroll into the $8,000 he sat down with. He told me later he couldn't believe how bad we played high-low.

He began winning right away and this pot came up after a few hours. Puggy, Moss, and I all had face cards. And Chip had a deuce up.

My hand was:

DOYLE

Chip had three baby hearts and Moss and Pug both had three-flushes. After sixth street, Puggy and Moss had both made ace-high flushes and I had caught two nines for a full house. Chip had a 6-4 already made for a cinch low and had a draw at a straight flush. The pot had been raised and capped on every street.

You can imagine the size of this pot!

On the river, chip made a wheel straight flush and scooped this pot. He told me later it had $29,000 in it. I'll leave it to Mike Caro to figure out how many bets were in that monster.

Chip went on to win $150,000 that night and never made it to law school. Instead, he became the best all-around poker player in the world. I've often wondered what his life would have been like if we hadn't been playing high-low split that night.

MEMORABLE
HAND #17

One of the most unbelievable feats in poker history was Stu Unger's first World Series win in the championship event. Stu had just come to Las Vegas a few months before and had won a lot of money playing gin rummy. He beat every top player in Vegas and made all of them quit. I'm convinced Stu knew something about gin rummy no one else ever figured out. He was far away the best gin rummy player ever. He also took those secrets to the grave when he overdosed on drugs in the late 1990s.

However, as talented a card player as Stu was, he hadn't played much poker and had never played no-limit hold'em when he entered the WSOP in 1980. He stumbled through the first day of the tournament. He had no concept of hold'em strategy and would have been eliminated if he had ever had any kind of hand beaten. But, he survived and got better and better as the tournament went on.

Finally, at the end of the four-day tournament it came down to me and Stu. I felt pretty confident I would beat him because of my experience. I was sure this was his first time he had ever played heads-up in any poker game. When we got two-handed, he had the chip lead almost 2 to 1. But I whittled him down to where we were even when this hand came up.

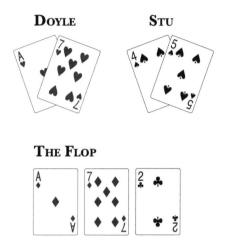

DOYLE　　　　**STU**

THE FLOP

I had raised this pot and Stu had called. There was $58,000 in the pot when I made a costly mistake. I bet $35,000, underbetting the pot and trying to suck Stu in. He called and when the 3♥ came on fourth street it made Stu a straight. Stu bet. I moved in all my chips and as he had the nuts, he called. The fifth card was no help and instead of me having my third championship, Stu had his first.

1980 WSOP Final Championship Hand

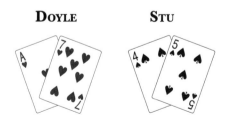

DOYLE　　　　**STU**

THE BOARD

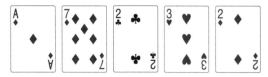

Stu went on to compile the most unbelievable tournament record ever. He was never a complete no-limit player in the cash games because he was such a steamer.

But, he will be remembered as the best tournament player in history.

MEMORABLE
HAND #18

In 1976, I wrote my first book on poker, *Super System*. There was a major uproar from many poker professionals who felt I gave away a lot of secrets that only a select few players knew. While that was true, the benefit the players got from the book far outweighed the negatives. The knowledge and strategies that were in *Super System* totally revamped poker as it was being played back then. It increased the number of players and contributed enormously to the popularity of the game.

One of the negative aspects of the book for me was that I had to completely change *my* game. I talked about aggressive play and how it was important to bet, bet, bet, and keep betting. I believed then, and still do, that is the most profitable way to play poker. I put my beliefs in the book, and since every serious poker player read *Super System*, they started calling and raising me to the point that I had to take a much more conservative approach to the game.

One such instance happened the year after the book came out. We were playing a big no-limit hold'em game at the Golden Nugget. Lyle Berman (the founder of the World Poker

Tour) and I were in a huge pot. I had raised. Lyle reraised, and I had reraised him. Then we saw the flop.

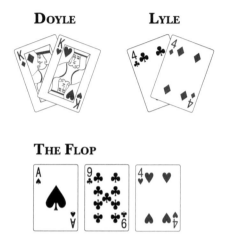

DOYLE   **LYLE**

THE FLOP

I checked. Lyle bet and I moved in on him, a very big bet! Lyle studied his hand a moment and then called. The turn and river cards were no help; and as Lyle was dragging in the pot, I said in a sad voice, "Didn't you think I might have three aces?"

Lyle stood up and screamed, "Doyle, I read your book!"

After a moment I realized what he was talking about. I say in my no-limit hold'em section, 'I never give a free card when an ace comes on the flop because unless the board is paired, the next card can always make a straight.' So Lyle knew I didn't have three aces. We have laughed about that many times since.

MEMORABLE
HAND #19

I've always said you have to keep your composure when you play poker. I've seen many a talented player go down in the poker world because they lost their cool in important situations. If you aren't right mentally—if you have women problems, business worries, or anything that keeps you from concentrating on your poker—you should wait and play another day.

We were playing no-limit hold'em when a very strange hand came up. I was in a pot with Joe Bernstein, a Poker Hall of Famer.

Joe had a history of being a very emotional player: He was a talented man, but he could get very distracted because of his personal life. This evening his girlfriend had stormed into the poker room cursing Joe and throwing things at him. After security had escorted her out of the casino, Joe sat back down to play.

Joe raised a pot with J♠ J♦. I called him with A♠ Q♠. The flop came J♣ 2♦ 2♥.

DOYLE   **JOE**

THE FLOP

Joe checked. I bet and Joe called. I thought he was weak and I was going to try to take the pot away from him. Shows you how wrong your feelings can be sometimes.

The fourth card was the 2♠.

THE TURN

I was almost dead. Joe checked and I bet again. Joe was sure I was bluffing so he just called. The fifth card was the 2♣.

DOYLE   **JOE**

THE RIVER

I had a cinch with my ace! Joe couldn't beat the board, but he didn't realize it and checked again. When I moved in he called and had to play the board. If he had been playing his usual game, he wouldn't have played so badly.

MEMORABLE HAND #20

I've learned when you are playing with amateurs you can take nothing for granted. When the World Series of Poker was in its infancy, we tried to start large cash games before the tournament started. If some unknown player would sit down with a lot of cash in front of him, the game would start and last for long periods of time. So when Jack Binion called me and told me a rich Texan named Rex wanted to have a $100,000 buy-in no-limit hold'em game, I rushed to the Horseshoe Casino to be sure I got a seat.

Sure enough, the game filled up and Rex was a real attraction. He obviously didn't know very much about poker and was losing horribly. I knew he had read *Super System*, because he kept quoting some of the things I had written. But Rex couldn't implement the knowledge I had given him.

We got into a heads-up pot. I had $250,000 in front of me and Rex had even more than that. I raised the pot with the 6♣ 5♣ and Rex called. The flop was K♠ Q♦ 3♥.

DOYLE   ### REX

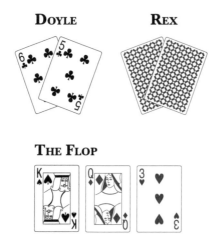

THE FLOP

THE RIVER

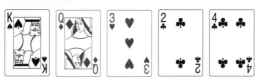

Rex checked. I wasn't about to bluff at a losing rich Texan so I checked, too. The next card was the 2♣. Rex checked and I checked behind him. The last card was the 4♣. The board looked like this:

I had a lock with a six-high straight, the best possible hand for this board! There was about $12,000 in the pot and Rex made a weak $10,000 bet. I reached for my chips and Rex grabbed his at the same time. It looked like he was ready to call a big bet. I knew he had read my book and might think I was trying to bluff him, so I raised him a very hefty $150,000.

I thought this man might have a heart attack. He looked at his cards, almost threw them away, looked back two or three times, and kept trying to muck his hand. Finally, shaking his head, he called. I turned up my 6-5 for a straight and he turned over a 6-5 also, tying me. I still had almost $100,000 in front of me and he hadn't raised me back.

What would you have thought?

The tragic part is that Rex went back to Texas, was involved in a drug deal, went to prison, and died there with over $100 million in a Ft. Worth bank. Greed can be a terrible thing!

MEMORABLE
HAND #21

When the World Poker Tour burst upon the scene a few years ago, poker soared to new heights in popularity. The WPT introduced the table mini-camera that allowed the TV audience an opportunity to see the players' hands. So, it was a special thrill for me to make the final table in the first WPT Championship Event at the Bellagio.

The Championship Event is a $25,000 buy-in with each player getting "double chips," or in other words, $50,000 in chips. This is five times the amount you get in most tournaments. And the players love it because it's a five day event, and the antes and blinds go up slowly. So there's more strategy involved than usual.

I had played very well the first four days and had gotten to the final table, the last six players. I had about $600,000 in chips and felt really good about my chances of winning. Unfortunately, the cards went sour on me and I couldn't make a hand. I stole enough chips to stay in the game, but my patience was wearing thin after three hours of bad cards. One player had been eliminated, so we were down to five.

Finally, a pot came up; and I must have made a bad read on Alan Goering, who was the chip leader at the time. The antes and blinds had gone up to where there was $50,000 in the pot before the cards were dealt. Alan was the first player to act. He took $30,000 worth of chips in his hand, hesitated for a moment and then reached back and got $30,000 more and opened the pot for $60,000.

I thought the slight hesitation was a sign of weakness, so I announced all-in, which was a raise of $440,000. I felt confident I would pick up the $110,000 that was in the pot. But I was horrified when Ted Forrest, a fine pro player said, "I call." Then, to compound my confusion, Alan also called with two jacks. Ted had called me with A-J. My hand was Q♠ 8 ♦.

DOYLE   **TED**   **ALAN**

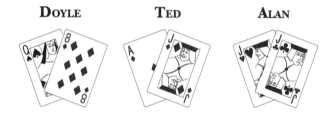

This is a classic example of playing your opponent, not your cards. My hand could have been 7-2 and I would have made the same play. Nobody got helped on the flop, turn or river, and Alan won the pot.

I've been criticized many times for making that play, but never from any of the top professional players. The pros understand I was playing my opponent, not my hand. There are times in a tournament when you can't catch a card, and the only way you're going to win chips and advance is to rely on your reading skills. Most of the time, if your reading ability is right on, it will work. Sometime, as in this hand with Alan, it won't.

I've actually won tournaments where I had bad streaks, so I guess I'll continue bluffing when I sense weakness.

MEMORABLE HAND #22

I was born and raised in a small farming community in West Texas called Longworth. It was a typical small town in the 30s and 40s. We were in the middle of the Bible Belt and everyone had strict moral values. Gambling was frowned upon, and many a preacher had his Sunday sermon on the evils of gambling. So, as you can imagine, I had no aspirations of ever becoming a professional gambler and had no knowledge of any kind of gambling as a youngster. But as you know, that would change.

I concentrated my efforts and energy into sports and succeeded in becoming an All-State basketball player. I also won the state championship in the mile run. If I hadn't had a serious injury to my leg, I would have played in the NBA (I was drafted by the Lakers). Instead, I was going to teach school using the master's degree I had received. So, in order to pay my college expenses, I started playing poker as a graduate student. I was doing well at the game and turned to poker to make my living. Soon, I was a professional.

Because poker and any form of gambling were considered

very wrong, I lied to my family and all my friends I grew up with because I didn't want to have the stigma of being a professional poker player.

You can imagine my surprise when, after Christmas dinner, my dad, my brother, and three of my uncles suggested we play a little poker. We were playing draw lowball with deuce-to-seven rules. My dad opened the pot for ten matches and I raised him twenty matches with a J-10-9-8-2. My dad called and stood pat. I had no hand to draw to, so I stayed pat behind him, thinking because he hadn't raised me back I could bluff him out of the hand.

Dad checked and I bet him the rest of my matches. Dad called. I said, "How in the world could you call that with a 10-8-6-4-2?"

Dad said, "I've been seeing plays like that for forty years."

After getting over my astonishment that he had said that, I began questioning him about how he knew anything about poker. Come to find out, Dad had put my brother and my sister through college playing poker at the Elks Club in Sweetwater, a town of 10,000 people about twelve miles from Longworth.

Sure enough, the apple didn't fall far from the tree!

MEMORABLE HAND #23

It is a common practice in the poker world to "stake" players. This means a person furnishes a player with the funds or money to play in a poker game. Many times it is done out of friendship, but not always. The money is commonly split 50-50 if the person being staked wins. I've seen other arrangements, such as 75-25, 60-40, and so on.

It was always my belief that if a player needed to be staked, it meant he was probably a losing player, so it would be a bad investment. That's not always the case because sometimes a winning player has bad habits such as sports betting, casino gambling, or just living too high for his bankroll. I have staked a few players usually out of friendship, but I rarely do it. When I'm worrying about what someone else is doing, it detracts from my own game.

I have had many offers from people who would want to stake me. I even had one pro who offered to furnish all the money I wanted if I would give him 15 percent at the end of one year. I refused it, because in fifty years of playing professionally, I've never had a losing year. So why give anything away? My feelings about this aren't shared by all my peers because some of them do take the deals. I guess I just have too much confidence in my poker playing.

The one time in my life I allowed anyone to stake me was when I was twenty-five years old. I was playing in a no-limit hold'em game in Brownsville, Texas, and had lost all my money to a bunch of amateurs who had been very lucky against me. The operator of the game, a friend named Skeet, threw me $200 to play on. I think he was afraid his game might break up. I played for several hours and had the money up to $1,800 when I got in a pot with Skeet.

I had two queens in my hand and the board was Q♦ J♦ 2♣.

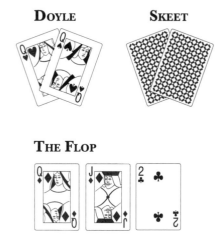

DOYLE   **SKEET**

THE FLOP

Skeet had A♦ 4♦ and I had raised him all my money and he was contemplating whether he would call or not.

Finally I told him, "Skeet, you staked me. I have the top trips."

He thought a minute and then said, "Hell, Doyle, I'll get half back if you beat me." He called, completed his flush and I left broke.

That was the end of letting someone else furnish my money.

MEMORABLE HAND #24

I was in Mobile, Alabama, playing no-limit hold'em right after my WSOP win in 1976. I had been invited to this private game in the middle of a swamp, which resembled some of the horror houses you see at Halloween. Most people don't know Mobile started Mardi Gras and has more witches and warlocks than any town in America. I felt completely out of place, but I had been told the game was great and greed is a powerful motivator.

There were some of the oddest-looking folks in this house I had ever seen. The people were dressed in spooky-looking attire. I thought at first it was a joke, but the guy that had invited me assured me it wasn't; that was the way they normally looked. There were also pictures of horses with men's heads and birds that looked like Satan himself.

The game was everything it was reported to be. All the players had a lot of money on the table and the action was unbelievable. The problem was that it was the most unfriendly game I had ever played in. There was none of the usual banter and small talk that goes on in every poker game. These guys were dead serious and looked like they wanted to drink your blood.

I was winning several thousand dollars and was being treated very rudely. I wanted to get up and leave but I was afraid it would start an uproar. I was in this pot with a particularly abusive player called Captain John, who supposedly was the captain of a riverboat that patrolled the Mississippi River.

DOYLE   CAPTAIN JOHN

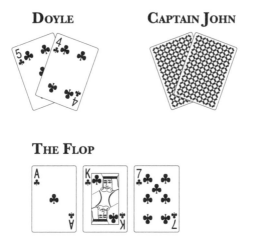

THE FLOP

Captain John bet. I called. The fourth and fifth cards were 2 ♦ and 6 ♥. The board looked like this:

THE BOARD

Captain John moved in. I remember it was in excess of $10,000. I studied a moment but the game was too liberal to throw a hand like this away, so I called.

Captain John called out "flush" without turning his hand over. I said, "That's good."

The Captain gave a victory spread and actually was laughing when he turned over the 3♣ 2♣.

As he reached for the pot I said, "I'm sorry. I have a 5-high flush. I just thought you had a better one."

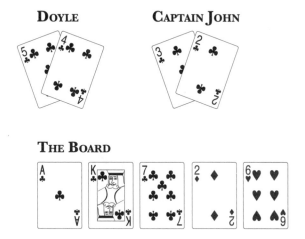

DOYLE

CAPTAIN JOHN

THE BOARD

The Captain's face turned red. He reached in his pocket, took out a knife and started around the table. Fortunately, another player stopped him before he got to me. I excused myself, took my $25,000 dollar win, and caught the first plane I could find back to civilization.

I never told anyone "That's good" again without seeing their hand. I suggest you don't either.

MEMORABLE
HAND #25

If you can't handle stress, you should stay away from poker. My family always asks me how I can take the pressure of high stakes gambling without it affecting me.

I do the best I can, then I don't worry anymore. It is a simple rule I live by in gambling, business, and everyday life. If you do your best, why agonize over it? I was probably broke one hundred times in my early years, but I didn't let it throw me. I've seen a lot of players literally age overnight because of bad hands and bad beats. You gotta let it go.

I was playing ace-to-five lowball with an elderly gentleman in Fort Worth, Texas, named Red Dodson. Red, as I recall, said his high school date to the senior prom was Ginger Rogers, the famous dancing partner of Fred Astaire.

We had played for several hours and Red was about the most conservative player I had ever seen. I kept bluffing at him and he kept throwing his hand away. I felt like Santa Claus had come early. Finally Red had a pat hand, A-2-3-4-6, the second best hand possible. I drew one card to an A-2-3-5 and caught a four, giving me the *best* possible hand. I bet, expecting Red to throw his hand away as he had done all night.

DOYLE

RED

To my surprise he moved in on me, yelling, "I know you have been bluffing me all night! Let's see what you do now!" I called. Red spread his 6-4 hand and then I showed my wheel.

His face turned white, his eyes rolled back, and then he began turning blue. He fell out of his chair and was dead before he hit the floor. The doctor said he had a massive heart attack. I felt bad, but that's poker and bad beats happen. You have to be able to handle them.

That was the second man I saw die at the table. Both were playing lowball. Maybe that's why hold'em became the game of choice.

MEMORABLE
HAND #26

I've always said you have to be alert around poker games. The more you watch, the more you learn about your opponents. You learn about their problems, their needs, and their overall disposition.

Puggy Pearson was the most alert person I have ever seen at the poker table. If he ever got tired, sleepy, or bored at the table he never showed it. He appeared to be incredibly intuitive, perhaps because he was so in tune with watching everyone. I tried to pattern myself after Puggy in that regard even though I felt he talked too much.

Shortly after I moved to Vegas, I was playing no-limit hold'em at the Dunes Hotel. If you don't remember the Dunes, it was sitting where the Bellagio is today. This was the one and only time I ever got to play with Nick "the Greek" Dandalos, the most famous gambler in the world at that time. I knew Nick's reputation as a very strong, aggressive player and I knew he was going to try to push me around. As I watched Nick, I marveled at his total disregard for money, and even though he was at the end of his career he was still a force to be reckoned with.

I remember in this one hand, I had 4♠ 4♣ and Nick had raised the pot. I called him. The flop was K♦ 7♦ 2♣.

DOYLE　　　**NICK THE GREEK**

THE FLOP

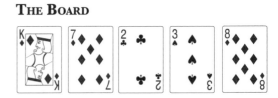

I was first so I checked. Nick made a large bet. I felt he was trying to push me out of the pot, possibly with a flush draw. I felt sure my fours were good so I called. The fourth card was the 3♠, which looked harmless. I checked. Nick bet again and I called. The last card was the 8♦, which would complete a flush if he had been drawing at it.

THE BOARD

I was watching Nick closely and he actually slumped in his chair when the last card hit. That made me think Nick thought I was drawing at the flush. I really thought he had nothing so I checked expecting him to bluff. After I checked, Nick must have felt I didn't have the flush and he moved in on me. I called him and he got up and quit the game without showing his cards. If I hadn't been alert I wouldn't have won that pot.

Nick left Las Vegas shortly after that. He was broke and was playing $5/$10 draw poker in California. A guy walked up and asked him if he wasn't embarrassed to be a famous gambler playing such cheap limits. Nick uttered one of the most famous lines in poker, "Action is action." He died shortly after.

MEMORABLE HAND #27

Back in Texas there was no organized crime like in the Eastern cities. Every town had its own 'boss gambler' who pretty much dictated how his town would be run. Some of the big crime families tried to infiltrate the rich Texas gambling market; but you know us Texans, we're too hardheaded to take orders from anyone.

I once asked Benny Binion if they ever tried to interfere with his business in Dallas. He told me, "They came, but they didn't leave."

In the 1950s and 1960s there was a man cut from the same cloth as Benny Binion. His name was Paul Harvey (no relation to the newscaster) and his town was Odessa, Texas. Paul ran the gambling in oil-rich Odessa in high fashion. He had a craps game at his house and he served the finest steaks in the world. He was also known for having the best quail dinners anywhere. If a good customer brought a female companion Paul gave her a full-length mink coat as a present. Imagine the clientele he had!

Paul was also an old rodeo cowboy. He was a grand physical

specimen, 6' 3" and 250 pounds, without an ounce of fat on him. They tried to rob his poker game once. Paul grabbed the pistol from one of the two gunmen and was shot in the neck while doing it. Then he and one of his employees named Tuffy proceeded to whip the two gunmen until they had to be taken to the hospital.

The reason I am telling you about Paul is that he ruled the poker game he ran with an iron fist. So when we were playing one night, Paul as usual was a big loser. We didn't have a dealer. We passed the deal around the table.

Paul picked the deck up, dealt everyone one card and stopped. We asked what he was doing and he replied, "This is one card lowball murder." "Murder!" he repeated. "No draw, just bet."

I looked at my card and it was the 4♠. I opened for about the size of the pot. Kingfish raised it and Paul moved in. I passed. Kingfish called and turned over a 3. Paul then turned over a deuce and won a huge pot.

That pot always stuck with me and it always reminds me: You have to be ready for almost everything at the poker table.

MEMORABLE HAND #28

Once the Internet poker sites became popular, unknown players were winning their real-world tournament seats online. Now, almost all the tournaments are filled with unknown players. While most of the players from the Internet aren't known, most of them are pretty good players because they have usually played many, many tournaments online. That puts me at a big disadvantage because they all know how I like to play, and most of them have read my books. And I, of course, don't know anything about them.

That wasn't the case in the early 1990s at the Four Queens Tournament in Las Vegas. After three days of play, the final table was me, Erik Seidel, T. J. Cloutier, Chip Reese, Berry Johnson, and Jack Fox. This was arguably the toughest final table ever. I knew it was the best players I had ever seen who had made it through a large field.

Berry went out quickly and Erik and Jack Fox played a strange pot, bluffing, re-bluffing, and finally Erik calling Jack's move-in. The third pair won the pot. (A third pair is when a player's hole card pairs with the third highest card on board.) That set the stage for the championship. I remember like it was yesterday.

The pot Erik had won gave him the chip lead and he handled it like the great pro that he is. He was taking control of the game against three of the top players in the world. Finally Chip got two kings and went all in against Erik's A-Q. Erik caught an ace to break him.

Then Erik really began to push T. J. and me around. I knew I was going to have to make a stand because nobody can make me keep throwing my hand away. Erik raised on the button, T. J. folded the small blind, and I looked down at 9♦ 2♦. I moved in. Erik, after a long study, called me with A♣ J♥.

I turned up my pitiful 9-2. T. J. laughed and said, "In Texas, we call that the Montana Banana."

I replied, "Well, it's close to the 10-2 I've been so lucky with." The flop was 10♥ 7♦ 3♦.

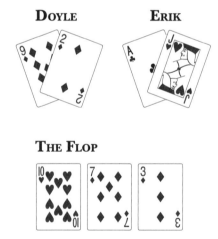

DOYLE   **ERIK**

THE FLOP

The fourth card was the 6♦ making my flush.

I went on to win the tournament but this hand reinforces what I've always said about tournaments: You need to play well, but you also need to get lucky at the right time.

MEMORABLE HAND #29

In 1969, when Tom Moore, a Texas gambler from San Antonio, bought the Holiday Inn in Reno, Nevada he had a tournament he called "The Texas Gamblers Convention." He invited all the high roller poker players he knew and it was a diverse collection of people.

Not many people realize the insular world a lot of the true gamblers live in. I remember "Corky" McCorquodale, one of the original inductees into the Poker Hall of Fame, asking me, "What is Vietnam?" This was almost at the end of the Vietnam War. Another well known pro asked me, "Is the Isle of Man close to the water?" Also he asked, "What language do they speak in London?"

This was the mentality of a lot of the players that came to Reno: not only the players from Texas but also those from other southern states. Great poker players? Yes. Well-rounded? No.

I was involved with one of these mental giants in a no-limit hold'em game. The Nevada pros were all there, but they were vastly inferior players in no-limit hold'em because the game was new to them. Aggression, however, was the common denominator in all these players: they all knew that to compete at these high levels, they had to be able to move their chips.

So when a hand came up between me and Tommy Abdo, another Hall of Famer, we both had one thing on our minds: Be aggressive! I had the 6♣ 5♣ and Abdo had the 5♥ 2♥. Someone else had raised the pot and we had called. The flop was K♣ 4♦ 3♥.

DOYLE   **ABDO**

THE FLOP

This gave Abdo and me open-end straight draws. The player who raised the pot bluffed at it. Abdo raised it. I thought I might win this pot right here so I moved in. Abdo was pot committed and called me after the other player passed. The fourth card was the 4♠ and the fifth card was the K♦.

THE BOARD

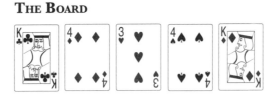

I won the pot with a 6-high. We counted the pot and it was over $100,000. That is still a lot of money, but in 1969 it was a fortune.

I'm sure that was the biggest pot ever won with a 6-high.

MEMORABLE HAND #30

It seems a lot of the hands I remember are from the old days, you know, right after the comet hit the earth that killed all the dinosaurs. I think it's because I played with inexperienced hold'em players.

The Texans brought hold'em to Las Vegas in the late 1960s. At that time and in the early 1970s, the biggest games were held at the old Dunes Hotel and Casino. The games were held there because all of the principle owners of the hotel were poker players. There was Sid Wyman, Bob Rice, Charlie Rich, Todd Durlocker, and Major Riddle.

The first four players I mentioned, while not all-star quality, were decent players and kept the games going.

The other player, Major Riddle, the largest shareholder of the Dunes, was a really bad player. When no-limit hold'em was introduced, all the Vegas players, along with the hotel owners, loved the game so much it replaced almost all of the other poker games. The players from the southern states came to Vegas and a lot of them left as rich men.

I was playing night and day in these games to be sure I got my part of the money that would no doubt be lost.

I was in a pot with Major Riddle and raised with A♦ K♦. Major reraised me and I called. The flop was K♥ K♠ 7♦.

DOYLE   MAJOR

THE FLOP

I checked. Major bet and I just called. I was 99 percent sure that I had the best hand and I didn't want to stop him from betting if he was bluffing. The next card was the 6♣ and I checked. Major bet and I called. The last card was the 7♠.

I checked again. Major bet and I moved in. Major quickly called and turned over 2♦ 2♥. He had the worst hand possible because there were two higher pairs on the board!

DOYLE   MAJOR

THE BOARD

No one could survive making mistakes like that. Major eventually lost all of his stock in the Dunes, then went down the strip and opened the Silverbird, where he proceeded to lose almost all of the fortune he had accumulated.

It was another sad Las Vegas story when Major died a few years later with a blood disorder.

MEMORABLE HAND #31

After seeing almost 9,000 players compete in the 2006 World Series of Poker, it seems strange to think about the event. For years it was the players that were willing to plunk down $10,000 to buy their seat. Then came the invention of satellites and super satellites where players could put down smaller amounts of money and win their seats.

Then Internet poker got so big almost half the field was from the different online sites. The sites developed online satellites, which became feeders to the main $10,000 WSOP event. It became possible for people anywhere in the world to win a seat for a small amount of money. Chris Moneymaker, who won the 2004 WSOP championship, had a total of $40 invested in an online tournament and ended up winning $2.5 million. The winner in 2006, Jamie Gold, won $12 million. He also came from the Internet.

Is it any wonder the Internet poker sites have prospered?

The poker hand I'm going to tell you about now was from a $1,150 satellite at the Horseshoe back in the early 1990s. I wasn't involved in the hand—I've always paid my entry fee to tournaments—but my son, Todd, was. It was down to him and Jack Keller, and I sat down to watch and root for Todd. The antes and blinds were advancing very fast and it was obvious it couldn't last long because both players were extremely aggressive.

Finally they got all in and turned over their cards.

TODD   **JACK**

THE FLOP

Both had flopped monster hands. Jack had the top two pair and Todd had a royal flush draw. The fourth card was the 10♦ giving Todd a royal flush. Jack was shaking Todd's hand, congratulating him, when the dealer turned the last card. It was the J♦.

THE BOARD

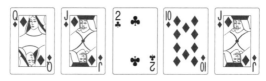

There were two J ♦ in the deck! I had never seen anything like that and still haven't to this day. The dealer called the floorperson and he had no choice but to call it a "no hand."

They resumed playing and Todd won anyway.

That hand exemplifies what Yogi Berra once said, "It ain't over till it's over."

MEMORABLE
HAND #32

I've always felt that the most underrated poker game is deuce-to-seven no-limit lowball. Deuce-to-seven is another poker game that was played all over the southern states and was brought west to Vegas at the same time as hold'em. Poker players in the western and eastern states played ace-to-five lowball and had trouble adjusting to the fact that in deuce-to-seven, straights and flushes count against you and an ace, being high, is weaker than a king.

In most no-limit games, the swing in money is severe because it is hard to have an opponent drawing dead so there is more hope to stay in the hand. In no-limit deuce-to-seven, that happens frequently. Because all hands are closed, players have less information and have to rely on instinct. Bluffing and position are also more important aspects of deuce-to-seven no-limit than any other game. The southern players filled their lock boxes very swiftly when this game gained popularity in Las Vegas.

We were playing at the Flamingo in the early years when a deuce-to-seven game was formed. It lasted for several days without stopping. Most of the local pros had already played and lost. The game was down to a group of tough lowball players. It might have been wise to quit, but I had always felt deuce-to-seven was perhaps my best game, so I stayed and played. And I was a big winner.

I got involved in a pot with Aubrey Day, a player from Alabama, who I considered to be the best player in the game. Aubrey was also a big winner and was playing very cautiously; at least I thought he was. I had the button and Aubrey was on my immediate right.

Aubrey opened the pot and I called. The manner and the amount of his bet made me feel he was drawing at a weak hand. I drew one at 8♠ 7♦ 3♦ 2♥ after Aubrey had drawn one.

AUBREY

DOYLE

I drew a 7♠ pairing my sevens and when Aubrey bet after the draw, I made a huge raise. Aubrey called immediately and then I said, "Take it."

He turned over a 10-9-8-6-2, which is a very weak hand, especially facing a raise.

AUBREY

DOYLE

I asked him later how he could call me. He said, "I knew you had a lot of gamble and thought I was weak, so I bet expecting you to raise." He had read me perfectly and my opinion of Aubrey Day, even though it was already high, went even higher.

It gave me another weapon to put in my arsenal—betting when you're expecting to get raised—and I still use it if the situation comes up.

MEMORABLE HAND #33

I get asked about Stu Unger more than any other modern day player. Stu died a few years ago from a drug overdose, and people are fascinated by his life story. He was a brilliant person with perhaps the quickest mind of anyone I have ever known. He was totally addicted to gambling and I'm sure his obsession to whatever he was playing carried over into his drug life.

Stu was the best winning player I ever played against, but unfortunately he was one of the worst losing players I've ever seen. He couldn't survive in the cash games because of this weakness; but in tournaments, his record will never be equaled. He entered thirty no-limit hold'em tournaments and won ten of them, including three World Championships at the WSOP. He also was the greatest gin rummy player the world has ever seen. Yet he couldn't overcome his personal demons.

I was playing no-limit hold'em with Stu the year before he died and this pot will tell you a lot about him. I had K♥ Q♥ and raised the pot. Stu reraised me trying to steal the pot right there. His hand was 8♥ 3♥. I called him because I knew the way he thought.

DOYLE   **STU**

THE FLOP

He bet and I raised him with the royal flush draw. Stu had a pair and a flush draw. Stu's hand couldn't be dead no matter what I had, so he moved in a monster bet. Obviously I had to call him and I turned my hand up and showed him I was drawing at a royal flush.

The pot was so huge I was prepared to lay "table insurance" or save some money if our hands were close. Stu turned over his hand and I felt this was a close hand so I offered to split the pot or at least take part of our money back.

Stu, who I knew was in desperate financial shape said, "No, let's gamble."

The turn and the river were blanks and Stu won the pot. I ran this hand on Mike Caro's Poker Probe. I don't remember which hand was the favorite but I know it was close. I've always respected Stu for his decision not to split that pot because that was his mindset.

'Let's gamble' describes Stu Unger perfectly.

MEMORABLE HAND #34

Before the Internet got poker sites that players could use as a training ground, quality players had to develop their poker skills in live cash games. There weren't any decent poker books out in the early 1970s so the serious players had to put in their hours at playing and analyzing hands to become world-class players. As most of the games were still in southern and midwestern states, there was a steady stream of "home town champions" that regularly came to Las Vegas to try their luck.

Most of these players weren't good enough to make it against the pros that had already made Las Vegas their home, but occasionally an exceptional player would show up. Such a player came to the 1974 WSOP. He was about twenty-five years old, very quiet, and a real southern gentleman.

I can't remember his real name but everyone that knew him called him "Waterhole." When I asked why, they told me his money was as hard to get as taking it out of a hole in the ground filled with water. After playing with him in several side games, I had to agree. This boy had a lot of talent.

We were down to twelve players in the main event when

this hand came up. Waterhole raised with two aces and I called with 6♠ 5♣. The flop was J♣ 6♦ 5♠.

DOYLE   **WATERHOLE**

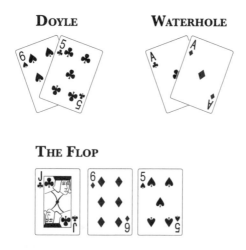

THE FLOP

We got all our money in right there. When the last card was a jack, I was eliminated.

The reason I remember this hand so well is because it was the last time I ever saw Waterhole. He was knocked out of the tournament that day and started driving back to his home in Texas. He stopped in Phoenix, went into a coffee shop in a hotel, ate breakfast, and went up to pay his bill.

He pulled several thousand dollars out into plain view as he searched for small bills to pay the check.

The cashier said, "You shouldn't carry so much money."

Waterhole said, "I don't have anything to do with it."

When the cashier said, "I wish I had that problem," he handed her all his money and said, "Now you have that problem."

He went out of the door, went to the top of the hotel, and jumped to his death.

I've wondered many times what could have happened in this young man's life to make him take such drastic measures.

MEMORABLE
HAND #35

In the 2006 World Series of Poker they had an event that I feel should become the main event. I say that because this event, which is called H.O.R.S.E., requires you to have more poker experience and card sense to play. The letters signify that five poker games would be played. The "H" is for hold'em, the "O" for Omaha 8-or-better, the "R" is for razz, the "S" for seven-card high and the "E" is for seven-card stud 8-or-better.

The cost for the H.O.R.S.E. event was $50,000, which made it the highest tournament entry fee in WSOP history. There were almost 200 players that entered this event and it was easily the most talked about tournament of the series.

We played thirty minutes of each game, changing games when we changed dealers. There is no room for one-game specialists in H.O.R.S.E. and the field narrowed quickly. Once the beginners and less experienced players were eliminated, the field toughened up and the days became very long. We played sixteen hours the first day. On the second day, we had to play down to the final table. We played for twenty hours more before we finally got down to the last nine.

Then, we were supposed to be back in nine hours for the final table. I was second in chips but a little tired after so many hours.

There were no strange faces at the last table when we started back up. This proved to everyone that this was an event that showed who the real poker players were. None of the Internet players survived this test.

My only objection was that no-limit hold'em was the only game played at this final table because ESPN wanted the TV audience to be able to follow the action. There were twenty-seven combined bracelet winners among those nine players.

I immediately became card-dead and my chips started dwindling away when this pot came up. I was first to act and the ante was $3,000 with $10,000 and $20,000 blinds. I had two black queens and I opened for $60,000. Chip Reese, who eventually was the winner, called, as did T. J. Cloutier and Phil Ivey.

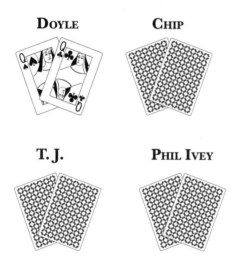

The Flop

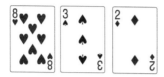

I bet $250,000 and Chip raised me $300,000. After thinking for a moment, I passed, as did T. J. and Phil. The TV cameras later showed Chip had two kings, which made my laydown look awesome. But I've played with Chip enough to know he wouldn't have even come into that pot with anything but two aces or two kings. We were the two chip leaders and he wasn't interested in playing a big pot with me. I should have realized it and not bet the $300,000 to begin with.

I get asked about that hand at every tournament I go to.

MEMORABLE
HAND #36

In the "Big Game" at the Bellagio, we usually play a cap of $100,000 per hand. This means you can only lose that amount in any one hand. We put this rule in effect because without a cap, vast sums of money would be won or lost on one hand and players would quickly go broke.

In no-limit, we play hold'em and deuce-to-seven, and in pot-limit, Omaha. Our limit games are usually deuce-to-seven triple draw, seven-card stud high, Omaha 8-or-better, razz, and seven-card stud 8-or-better. We usually play these games $4,000/$8,000 so you see the parity of the $100,000 cap. The cap puts a different strategy in the pot-limit and no-limit games because of the high ante that is in effect—you have to play more hands to be successful and the high limit player likes the action.

But for some reason, at the 2004 WPT championship event at the Bellagio, we were playing with no cap. All the high rollers were in town and the game was going around the clock. It seems that the bigger the event, the bigger the games become. We were playing no-limit hold'em when this hand came up between Lyle Berman, the founder of the World Poker Tour, and me.

I held the K♣ Q♣ and had raised the pot. Lyle called. The flop was A♣ 10♣ 4♥.

DOYLE   LYLE

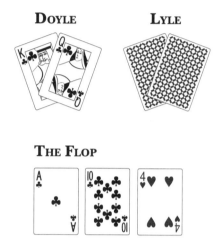

THE FLOP

I made a big bet at the pot and Lyle called. The fourth card was the J♠ making me the nut straight. Lyle held the K♥ Q♥ giving him the same straight. However, I had four clubs for a total freeroll.

I led out with a big bet and Lyle made a huge raise. After a moment, I hoped Lyle had the same straight as I had and would have to call any amount if I raised, so I moved in. Both of us had well over $600,000 in front of us at this time. Lyle had to call but commented as he put his money in the pot, "I hope you don't have the king and queen of clubs."

The last card was "Jim Miller," poker players' pet name for the lowest ranking card in the deck, the deuce of clubs.

The deuce completed my flush and I won one of the largest pots in my career.

MEMORABLE HAND #37

One advantage of playing online poker is that it eliminates dealer mistakes. There is nothing as aggravating as a dealer who makes a mistake that costs you a lot of money. Another advantage is that online, more hands per hour get dealt which makes it more profitable for good players—and for the house. These concepts are behind Poker Tech, a new idea for poker rooms which features computer screens in front of each player. The hands are automatically dealt just like online. A big advantage of Poker Tech over online play is that you can actually see your opponent and try to read him.

We were playing in a big deuce-to-seven no-limit lowball game at the Flamingo Hotel. There was some gaming convention in Las Vegas when this game started and, as most games do when the action is fast and big, had been going on for days. The action was soft because of the players from the convention. The local pros were swarming around them like a pack of hyenas, trying to get into the game. All the big games revolve around who is in town at the right time and this game was no exception.

A tough pro from Tennessee named James (Goody) Roy and I had started the game and we were on our third day without stopping. Both of us were winning big and were determined to stay as long as the weak players were there. As in most cases like this, I wasn't looking to play big pots with Goody or he with me. We were looking to get into the pots with the weaker players.

I had just lost a couple of pots to this guy from Illinois and I was a little hot under the collar. This player was raising every pot and was playing very fast. The dealer started dealing and I did something I almost never do. I looked at each card as it was dealt to me. I looked at 2-3-5-7 and got very excited. I squeezed the last card and it was a 4 giving me an unbeatable hand. To my horror, the dealer kept dealing, and before I could stop him he had dealt six cards, making the hand a misdeal.

Goody let out a scream, turning over 2-3-4-6-7, the second best hand. I would have won all his money. Instead I was so disgusted I got up and quit.

Where was Poker Tech when I needed it?

MEMORABLE
HAND #38

In the second WSOP we had an event called high-low split regular. That meant it was seven-card stud and the best high hand and the best low hand would split the pot. There was no declare and no qualifier, which made it more important to go for the low hand and let the high hand take care of itself.

For example, if you had three kings the first three cards, you should throw your hand away when a low card raised that pot and it was just you and he left. The reasoning was that it was almost impossible for you to win all of the pot and it wasn't worth the investment you had to make for only half the pot. There were no poker books out at this time and in order to play this game, a player had to rely on his card sense and experience. I had played high-low regularly in college so I felt I had a big advantage on the field when we started.

After we played for a while, it became obvious most of the participants hadn't played this game much and the field narrowed quickly. Early into the second day there were only two of us left, myself and David Sklansky. David was to become one of the best poker authors in the world. He was a very good player and we sparred for several hours before this hand came up.

My hand was A♥ 2♣ 5♠ 8♦. David's hand was 4♠ 5♦ 7♥ 8♥.

DOYLE   **DAVID**

I was startled when David kept raising me. I had the best low draw and my ace was good for high. I couldn't understand it and I raised until David was all in. I made my low when I caught the 4♠ and I won high when I made two eights. David completely busted out, catching 10, J and K. So I won the tournament!

Later, I read an article David wrote for a magazine and he had this to say: "I knew at that moment I know more about high-low regular than Doyle." He went on to explain how his hand was the favorite because of the straight draw and if he paired, they would be bigger than my pair. After consulting some mathematicians, I discovered his hand really was a small favorite. I knew I had better do my homework on the math in poker.

I also liked the way David ended his article by saying, "… but Doyle wasn't giving any refunds."

MEMORABLE HAND #39

I've always said I thought Johnny Moss was one of the greatest players I've ever seen. Johnny was about fifty years old when I first started playing against him, and he had uncanny ability when he was playing no-limit games. When he was about sixty, he came to Vegas. While John was still a great no-limit player, his limit game was very suspect because he had never played much limit poker. At that point Johnny began to go downhill with his poker playing; and even though he played another twenty-four years, he was very poor at the end and Las Vegas never saw Johnny Moss when he was great.

There was another great player from Oklahoma named George Barnes. George came to Vegas when the poker games became big in Nevada. I didn't like seeing him move to Vegas because I had played a lot with him in the south and I knew he would be tough competition. It had been three to four years since I had played with him, and George was in his early sixties when this hand came up in a no-limit hold'em game.

It was a raised pot and I had the J♦ 10♦. George had the A♣ K♣ and the flop was J♥ 10♣ 4♣.

DOYLE　　　**GEORGE**

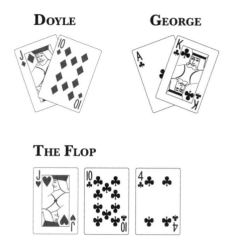

THE FLOP

This was a terrific flop for both of us. I remember looking at George's chips and noticing he had about $50,000 in front of him, matching my stack. I knew how aggressive George usually was, so I bet right out. George called. The turn was the 2♥. I bet again and George called. The river was the 6♦.

THE BOARD

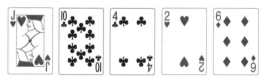

I checked because I thought George might bluff at the pot. However, he checked, showed the A♣ K♣ and said, "Nice hand." He got up and quit the game. I felt a moment of sadness at that point because I could see that he wasn't the same player I had played with before. The George Barnes I knew would have been all in on the flop. He had lost his courage.

I had always heard that poker players start to lose their ability when they pass fifty years of age, and I believe that is true. I feel very fortunate to still be playing at the highest level at the age of seventy-three. I think the secret is to stay mentally active; and of course, you gotta have good genes.

Sometime later that year George had a flat on the freeway and was hit by a car and killed as he was changing the tire. He was one of the best "unknown" players I ever played against.

MEMORABLE
HAND #40

I've never cared much for Omaha high, even though it has become more and more popular—especially in Europe. Most Omaha games are pot-limit and the fluctuation is very high, with a number of hands being coin flips; this means both hands are about equal and because of the money already in the pot, it is correct for both players to put the rest of their money in. I prefer games where it's much harder to draw out on the best hand, like hold'em and seven-card stud. Omaha 8-or-better high-low split, however, is one of my favorite games.

Occasionally, in the big game at The Bellagio, Omaha is played with a set limit like $4,000/$8,000. This makes it a bigger crapshoot because everyone stays to the last card and there are lots of drawouts.

We were playing limit Omaha and I had A♥ K♥ 5♦ 4♦, which is a decent starting hand. The flop was 6♠ 6♦ 3♦.

DOYLE

FLOP

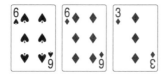

I was in the pot with Jennifer Harmon and Eli Elezra, two world-class players who were both losers and really gambling. They raised the limit of raises, which meant we put $20,000 each into the pot on the flop. I figured Jennifer and Eli both had a 6 in their hand with big kickers.

With my open-ended straight flush draw, I thought I was in a good position to bet, since neither of my opponents had a full house. The fourth card was the 3♣, which looked like a perfect card because someone had to have quads or the perfect 6 and 3. Sure enough, after five more raises of $8,000, we had put another $40,000 each into the pot. The pot was now well over $200,000, which was almost a new record for this limit.

The last card was the 2♦, making my straight flush.

BOARD

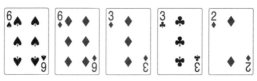

Eli bet, I raised and Jennifer passed. To my surprise, Eli only called and showed me a 6 and a 3. The only thing that could beat him was the 5♦ and 4♦, and that's what I had. When I asked him why he didn't raise he simply said, "The pot was big enough for me."

I violated a cardinal rule in poker, especially Omaha poker, when I drew at a flush with a pair on the board. It shows you that it helps to be lucky sometimes.

MEMORABLE HAND #41

Regardless of what anyone says, the number one poker tournament in the world is the main event at the World Series of Poker (WSOP). There are other very prestigious tournaments but none rival the WSOP. I had won the championship twice and really wanted that third win to catch my poker idol, Johnny Moss. In 1980, I had been second to Stu Unger and in 1982, I had been fourth, so I was really playing well.

It was 1983 and we were on our fourth grueling day. I had the chip lead at the final table. I felt the only real threat to me was Carl McKelvey, an old Texas circuit player and Donnacha O'Dea, a former Olympic swimmer from Ireland. After Donn was knocked out in sixth place, McKelvey took a bad beat and was eliminated in fourth place.

I could just taste my third championship. I was left with two virtually unknown players, Rod Peate and Tom McEvoy. I knew Rod was a limit hold'em player from Los Angeles and that Tom had been playing for a very short time. However, I was also aware that my play against players who were inexperienced hadn't been as good as it was when I was playing tough opponents. I was determined to play carefully and not take this tournament lightly at this point.

I had a 2-1 chip lead over Tom and Rod when the dreaded "no-cards" hit me. I couldn't win a pot and both Rod and Tom picked up on that and began to push me around by betting and taking pots that I ordinarily would have won. So I decided I would have to straighten these kids out and get aggressive.

I picked up the J♦ 9♦ in a raised pot. The flop was 9♣ 3♦ 2♦.

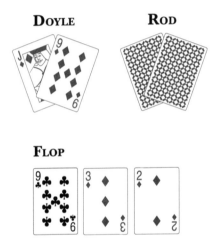

DOYLE   **ROD**

FLOP

Rod Peate made a small bet at the pot and I thought he was stealing. Even if he did have a legitimate hand, my hand was very strong with the top pair and four diamonds. So I moved in on him. To my dismay, Rod said, "I've got the top trips" and turned over the other two nines.

DOYLE **ROD**

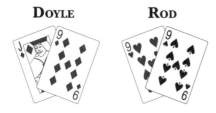

No diamond came and I had to settle for third place instead of my third win.

MEMORABLE
HAND #42

I've always been a stickler for rules and try to observe them. If a situation comes up when I'm playing poker—even if the floorman rules in my favor—I make it a point to ask: "If my name was John Smith would you make the same ruling?" I don't expect, nor do I want, any favoritism just because I've been around for a long time. I think most rules are made for a purpose and have to be strictly enforced to be effective.

There are exceptions to good rules, however, and they should be taken out of the cardrooms' rulebooks.

One of these rules caused me a lot of problems at a tournament at the old Frontier Hotel. This particular rule says that if you can't beat what you're looking at, then you can take the money back from your last call. The rule was put into effect to protect a player who accidentally calls when he can't beat his opponent's upcards. It is an even worse rule for seven-stud games than five-stud because most seven-stud players have never heard of it. Most of the old-time five-stud players, however, are very aware of it.

The hand I remember was in a five-card stud tournament.

I was in a pot with an amateur named Alex, who wasn't familiar to me, and I was having trouble figuring out his style.

His upcards were A♠ 10♦, 4♣ and 2♣. I had an ace in the hole and my upcards were 9♣ 7♠ 3♦ 2♠.

DOYLE

ALEX

So, when Alex moved in, I obviously knew I couldn't win. But I was curious about his hole card, so I called his bet. When he turned a 9 out of the hole, showing me he was bluffing, I said, "That's good," and took my last bet back. Alex screamed and called me names after the rule was explained to him. I told him I was sorry; I was only abiding by the rules, but he never forgave me for doing that.

Truthfully I don't blame him and I never did that again.

MEMORABLE
HAND #43

At the World Series of Poker, when someone wins an event the player receives a gift: a nice gold bracelet. This was started in 1971 and is a tradition that is still observed. I won several events back in the 1970s and 1980s and didn't put any particular significance to getting the bracelets.

But as time passed, a highly publicized contest evolved between myself, Johnny Chan and Phil Hellmuth, that's been dubbed, "The Battle of the Bracelets." I never dreamed it would come to be so important to win those bracelets or I would have played more tournaments. Most years I only played in lowball, seven-stud, and the championship no-limit hold'em tournaments. I didn't wear jewelry and gave the bracelets to family members as fast as I won them. In fact, I think, one year I didn't even pick one up when I won it.

Later as the media made the bracelets so important, everyone started playing more events. Johnny Chan, Phil Hellmuth, and I had nine bracelets each and everyone was watching us closely in 2005. Then Chan won a no-limit hold'em tournament and got his tenth. I watched him win it with mixed feelings, but I was actually pulling for him because I knew someone had to do it. Phil and I both congratulated him and we both resolved in our heart to catch him.

Two weeks later in the six-handed no-limit hold'em tournament, I found myself at the last table. There were six very good players there, and I watched as they were eliminated one by one until it was just Ming Ly and myself left. I had played a lot with Ming, and I knew how tough he could be.

I had a pretty nice lead on him but the antes and blinds had gotten so big your chips could literally evaporate. So when Ming had the button and didn't raise, I had a strong feeling he was weak. I moved in on him, and to my surprise he called and turned over K♦ Q♠. My hand was an awful 10♦ 3♥.

Ming said, "What you have, 10-2?"

I laughed, turned over my hand and said, "No, I've got his big brother."

DOYLE   **MING**

THE FLOP

The flop gave me two 3s. The fourth and fifth cards were no help and I won my tenth bracelet.

As I write this, Phil Hellmuth has won his tenth in 2006 and Johnny and I were shut out, so there is a three-way grid lock. I can't wait for the 2007 WSOP.

MEMORABLE HAND #44

I consider poker to be a sport. And a recent poll of poker players across the country reinforces that opinion. There are so many of the same elements found in sports and poker. Dedication, discipline, patience, endurance, and love of your game are a few of the similarities.

As an ex-athlete, I know that there is always someone who gives you more trouble than anyone else. When I was in college there was a player who played for Oklahoma named Arnold Short. I was considered a top defensive player but I couldn't stop this guy from scoring. In track I was one of the top milers in the nation but UTEP had a Mexican named Xavier Montez, who I never beat.

Were they better than me? Perhaps. But not to the extent that they dominated me.

My Achilles heel in poker has always been Chip Reese. I know Chip is a great player but it seems he wins 80 or 90 percent of the pots I play against him. No player in my lifetime has ever intimidated me except Chip. I'm not really superstitious, but I've done everything I know to do against him. I've varied my game to where I know it is impossible for him to get a read on how I'm playing.

This was one of the first hands I remember playing against him when he first came to Las Vegas from Dartmouth College. We were playing no-limit hold'em and Chip and I were left alone. I held the A♦ J♦ in a raised pot.

The flop was 9♦ 7♥ 2♠.

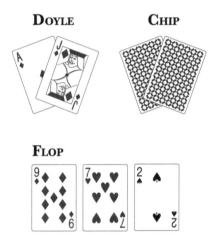

DOYLE　　　　**CHIP**

FLOP

I checked and Chip checked. The next card was the Q♦ giving me the nut-flush draw. I checked. Chip bet and I thought he was weak so I raised. He called and the river was the 3♠.

I moved in and he called me. It was a very big pot for the game we were playing and he turned over the 5♦ 2♦. He had called me with two deuces!

DOYLE　　　　**CHIP**

THE BOARD

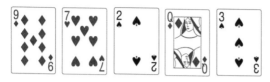

He made the call because he put me on a busted flush draw and figured I had nothing. I asked him later what he would have done if a diamond had come, which would have given him a flush but me a bigger one. He told me he would have thrown his hand away. How do you handle that?

That was thirty years ago and I'm still trying to find the answer.

MEMORABLE HAND #45

The year 2004 had been a hard one for me. I had a gastric bypass operation and wasn't feeling too good at the WSOP. The cash games were better than they had been in years, and I was playing in them instead of the tournaments. I wasn't playing well and was also playing very unlucky.

I got loser, and instead of taking a break like I usually do when I go on an extended losing streak, I kept playing and I lost the staggering sum of $6 million.

I was a little winner for the year but this seemed to be an insurmountable deficit to overcome. I was faced with making a difficult decision. I was seventy years old. Had I lost it? The brightest of stars fade with time. Should I retire? Those thoughts were on my mind as I went to my second home in Montana to rest and decide what to do. I stayed in Montana for a month pondering this.

I felt fine after that respite and decided I would go play the WPT event at the Bicycle Club in Los Angeles that was about to begin and avoid the cash games. I was interviewed by a national TV network and told them I felt I had something to prove for the first time in almost fifty years. This was the largest WPT circuit event to date with almost 700 players entered.

The first few days I played as well as I had ever played in my life. I made the final table but Lee Watkinson had a massive chip lead. It finally came down to Lee and I, but he had a 3-1 chip lead. I played very lucky to win a couple of big pots and actually took the lead when this hand came up. I had the Q♥ 9♥. The flop was Q♦ J♠ 4♣.

DOYLE **LEE**

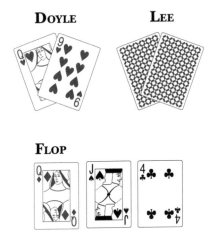

FLOP

I knew Lee had to be steaming, and if he had any kind of a draw he was going to bet. So I checked. He bet $400,000 and I raised him $2.5 million.

Lee said, "I call," and turned over the Q♣ 3♣. The next card was an A♣, which gave Lee lots of cards to tie my hand. But, the last card was the 8♥ and I had my first WPT championship.

DOYLE   **LEE**

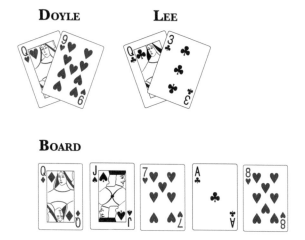

BOARD

I felt great about my win because I was the first WSOP champion to ever win a WPT event. I also started winning again in the cash games, which was more important.

MEMORABLE HAND #46

I am very fortunate to have a great sense of recall; that is why I can write this book. I remember hands clearly from my training days back in Ft. Worth through my years on the Texas Circuit, and after, when I moved to Las Vegas. I learned things every step of the way and I am still learning. That's why poker is such a great game.

When I first came to Vegas, the biggest hold'em games were played at the Golden Nugget in downtown Las Vegas. I was an outsider and didn't know exactly how to handle the blatant cheating that was going on.

One of the main culprits was Bill Douglas, a personable young man from the Midwest. He had been a fixture in the Vegas poker rooms for years and I couldn't understand why he was allowed to stay. Fortunately, Bill watched me and liked the way I played, so he stayed out of my games. Amarillo Slim was with me and had known Bill from his pool-playing days.

So if Bill was in a game, I stayed out of it, and if I was in a game, Bill stayed out. The one exception was when the game was limit and both of us would play. I figured if he did cheat, it wouldn't be too expensive and I could quit if I wanted.

It doesn't have to be a huge pot to be memorable; it doesn't even have to be a big one. But you'll see in a minute why this hand makes the book.

We were playing $10/$20 limit hold'em. It was a great game with all the Nevada players participating. They were inexperienced at hold'em.

Bill had just won a huge pot with a royal flush. I wasn't involved in this pot, but I was sitting next to him and he was laughing about all the money that was in that pot. The next pot I had the small blind and Bill had the big blind. It was raised and I had 7-6 suited so I called as did Bill. The flop was A♠ K♠ 10♠. I checked. Bill bet and everyone went out including me.

What makes me remember that hand?

Bill said, "There's another one." He flashed me his hand as he threw it away, and so help me it was the Q♠ J♠ for another royal flush. I have always wondered if there was some kind of cheating going on that I didn't see.

Two royal flushes in a row? Unheard of! Anyway, I played a few minutes longer, felt uncomfortable and got up and quit.

# MEMORABLE HAND #47

After I left Ft. Worth in the late 1950s and started traveling the Texas Circuit, one of the hazards was the Texas Rangers. Poker was illegal in those days and despite the efforts of local gamblers to make their poker games safe, the Rangers seemed to know where the games were and would come and arrest the operators and often the players as well. If we were arrested and charged with a misdemeanor, we paid a fine and then would be set free.

The operators of the games would often be charged with a felony, which meant they could be tried and sent to jail if convicted. One of the Rangers was a captain named Jim Riddle and was known to all of us as "Cap" Riddle. We had been arrested by Cap several times and had come to know him as a firm but fair man. The local authorities could be persuaded to look the other way, but as far as I knew, the Rangers were incorruptible.

We were playing in a farmhouse outside of Midland, Texas, one night. I was having a horrible night, one that every poker player experiences every so often. We were playing half no-limit hold'em and half no-limit deuce-to-seven. Every hand I had the entire night was beat by one of the circuit players.

The hold'em hands I had lost were brutal but the deuce-to-seven hands were even worse. I had drawn at quality hands all night long and had paired almost every time.

We were in a lowball game and I had opened the pot. Bill Smith, a West Texas player who would later win the championship event at the WSOP, moved in on me for a huge raise. Ordinarily, I would probably have passed, but I was steaming from losing so many pots. I had a 7-4-3-2, a draw to the best possible hand, but still a nice underdog to a pat hand, which I was pretty sure Bill had.

Just as I put all my money in the pot, the door was smashed in and the Rangers came in with drawn weapons. Captain Riddle was the first one to the table and told us to put our hands up. I knew they weren't going to shoot us, and I said to Cap Riddle, "Can I see if I was going to make this hand?"

He smiled and said, "Go ahead."

I got the deck, burned one and looked at the next card. It was a 5, making me the perfect hand.

It just wasn't my night.

MEMORABLE HAND #48

One of the questions I get a lot concerns which one of the young players is the best. There are a lot of good players out there, but my answer is always the same, "Come back in twenty years and see who is still here."

I have seen many, many talented young guys that have put up good results for a year or two. Then something will happen and they seem to vanish. Hometown champions are what the top pros are waiting for. Playing poker for a living is a lot harder than people think, although the many tournaments available make it more likely that an average player can be successful.

After the turn of the century, one of the names I kept hearing was Phil Ivey. Phil is from Philadelphia and is certainly one of the most talented young players. I consider anyone under thirty-five to fall into the "young" category. He had won three WSOP events in one year, which is a remarkable achievement. I knew he was a strong all-around player but I had doubts about his no-limit hold'em. Phil moved right into the biggest game in Las Vegas and was doing well. I watched him closely and I was impressed by his ability and even more by his demeanor at the table. Nothing seemed to rattle him and that is a big factor in a top poker player.

We were in the middle of an extra big game at the Golden Nugget in the 2003 WSOP. We were playing the regular limit of $4,000/$8,000 but in no-limit we were playing with a $2,000 ante, $3,000/$6,000 blinds and a $200,000 cap. I was on the button and everyone had passed around to me. I opened for $20,000 and Phil raised me $40,000. I had two black aces and thought Phil might be making a play because I had the button so I just called.

The flop was 8♣ 3♦ 2♠.

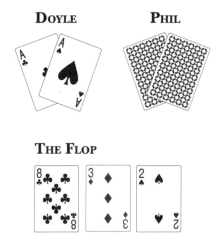

DOYLE   **PHIL**

THE FLOP

Phil bet $60,000. I just called again because I thought he was bluffing. Phil had the K♦ Q♦ and the turn was the K♣. Phil moved in and I called. We turned over our hands with one card to come and I was really pleased with the way I had played this hand. However, the last card was the Q♣ making Phil two pair. He gave me a sheepish glance as he raked in that $400,000 pot.

DOYLE   **PHIL**

THE BOARD

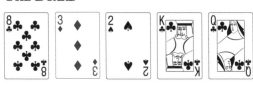

I told him, "Don't worry, son, you and I will play a lot of pots before I'm gone."

We have and we will!

MEMORABLE HAND #49

Since Harrah's took the WSOP over when they bought out Binion's Horseshoe, the "bracelet race" has escalated. In order to take advantage of this craze, there will be sixty events in the 2007 World Series. I personally think that cheapens the bracelets, but it is such a financial windfall for Harrah's you can't really blame them. Most of the tournaments are hold'em events, both limit and no-limit. I would like to see different games, but because of the TV coverage the past few years, hold'em is the most popular and gets more entries.

In the 2006 WSOP, everything was over except the main event and it was in its third or fourth day. Out of nowhere, the tournament directors decided to have one more $1,000 hold'em tournament. Ordinarily I would have never even considered playing in this event, but the fact that Phil Hellmuth, Johnny Chan, and I were tied for the all-time bracelet lead with ten each, made me decide to enter. It was a one day event and I knew if I made it to the final table and beyond it would be a twenty-hour day. It had already been a long, tiring six weeks since the WSOP had started.

There were over 500 players who entered, including Chan and Hellmuth. I played very cautiously for the first few levels because I was determined to go deep in this tournament. I was lucky enough that I won a few pots early and I could afford to play the waiting game. Chan was knocked out early but Hellmuth had a lot of chips and I wanted to challenge him.

Phil is a hold'em specialist in the tournaments and probably plays bad players better than anyone in the world. I knew he would be around and was a definite threat to win.

There was a player who was drinking and making all kinds of noise. Everyone was hoping to get to his table because he was playing recklessly and looked like he was a cinch to go broke.

I was holding a few hands and with three tables left I was the chip leader and Hellmuth was second. My table was down to five players and was broken up, leaving two tables. I moved to the same table with Phil and the player who was drinking, but who had the third biggest stack in the tournament.

The first hand I caught the A♥ 10♦ and brought it in. The drunk called and the flop was A♦ 7♥ 9♦.

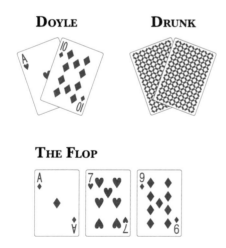

DOYLE   **DRUNK**

THE FLOP

I made a big bet and the drunk moved in. I knew my hand was pretty weak, but I also knew this player was going to throw his chips away. I felt if I could win this pot, I had an excellent chance to win my 11th bracelet, so I called.

The drunk turned over A-K and won the pot. This crippled me so badly that I went broke shortly after. Phil came over and shook my hand and I could see the relief in his eyes that I was out.

Hellmuth went on to finish third to set up an interesting scenario for the 2007 WSOP.

MEMORABLE
HAND #50

I've always been partial to cash games over tournaments. Tournaments have caused a big decline in cash games because the media has made them so popular. In order to be a real poker player, I think you need to play for whatever money you put in a pot, not just whatever the tournament buy in was.

If you are going to be a professional poker player, the cash games are your bread and butter. The tournaments are so big these days that you can go into extended droughts playing in them. I've won twenty-five tournaments but most of them have been almost "accidental" wins because there was no action outside of the tournament.

Back when Amarillo Slim had his Super Bowl of Poker tournament, we were snowed in at Lake Tahoe. The side games were terrific because no one could leave. We had been playing steadily for a week and I hadn't played in any of the small tournaments.

Then one day I got up and there was no cash game going so I entered a no-limit hold'em tournament. I was doing pretty well when the most unbelievable deuce-to-seven no-limit game started. I could see it was going to be several hours before this tournament was going to be over and I thought my expectations in the cash game far outweighed the tournament.

So I ran over to the cash game, put my money down, and started playing. I was forfeiting my antes and blinds but I would run back to my seat in the tournament and make a ridiculous play. But miracle after miracle would happen, and I would win and build my chips up. Then I would go back to the cash game and play for a while, then run back to the tournament.

This went on for a few hours and I kept winning in both games. Finally, the tournament was down to three tables. I went to my seat and picked up the K♠ Q♠. At last, a legitimate hand!

I raised the pot. My good friend and neighbor Chau Giang moved in and I called him. Chau had two sevens and the flop was K-7-2.

DOYLE   **CHAU**

THE FLOP

I got up to leave but the turn was a 2 and the river was a king, giving me kings full and enough chips to give up my seat in the cash game. I went on to win the tournament.

I got over $100,000 in cash for my win and also won a Chevrolet Blazer and a matching set of silver-plated shotguns.

FROM CARDOZA'S EXCITING LIBRARY
ADD THESE TO YOUR COLLECTION - ORDER NOW!

SUPER SYSTEM by Doyle Brunson. Jam-packed with advanced strategies, theories, tactics and moneymaking techniques, this classic work,widely considered to be the most important poker book ever written! Chapters are written by six superstars: Mike Caro, Chip Reese, Dave Sklansky, Joey Hawthorne, Bobby Baldwin, and Doyle—two world champions and four master theorists and players. Essential strategies, advanced play, and no-nonsense winning advice on making money at 7-card stud (razz, high-low split, cards speak, declare), lowball, draw poker, and hold'em (limit and nolimit). A must-read—every serious poker player must own this book. 628 pages, $29.95.

SUPER SYSTEM 2 by Doyle Brunson. The most anticipated poker book ever, SS2 expands upon the original with more games and professional secrets from the best players in the world. Superstar contributors include Daniel Negreanu, winner of multiple WSOP gold bracelets and 2004 Player of the Year; Lyle Berman, 3-time WSOP gold bracelet winner and founder of the World Poker Tour; Bobby Baldwin, 1978 World Champion; Johnny Chan, 2-time World Champion and 10-time WSOP bracelet winner; Mike Caro, poker's greatest researcher, theorist, and instructor; Jennifer Harman, the world's top female player; Todd Brunson, winner of more than 20 tournaments; and Crandell Addington, no-limit legend. 672 pgs, $34.95.

CARO'S BOOK OF POKER TELLS by Mike Caro. One of the 10 greatest poker books, this must-have classic should be in every player's library. If you're serious about winning, you'll realize that most of the profit comes from being able to read your opponents. This book reveals the the secrets of interpreting *tells*—physical reactions that reveal information about a player's cards—such as shrugs, sighs, shaky hands, eye contact, and more. Learn when opponents are bluffing, when they aren't and why—based solely on their mannerisms. Over 170 photos of poker players in action and play-by-play examples show the actual tells. These powerful eye-opening ideas can give you the decisive edge at the table. 320 pages, $24.95.

CARO'S GUIDE TO DOYLE BRUNSON'S SUPER SYSTEM by Mike Caro. Working with World Champion Doyle Brunson, the legendary Mike Caro has created a fresh look to the "Bible" of all poker books, adding new and personal insights that help you understand the original work. Caro breaks 36 concepts into the following categories: analysis, commentary, concept, mission, play-by-play, psychology, statistics, story, or strategy. Lots of illustrations and winning concepts give even more value to this great work. 86 pages, 8 1/2 x 11, $19.95.

CARO'S FUNDAMENTAL SECRETS OF WINNING POKER by Mike Caro. Learn the essential strategies, concepts, and plays that comprise the very foundation of winning poker play. Learn to win more from weak players, equalize stronger players, bluff a bluffer, win big pots, where to sit against weak players, and the six factors of strategic table image. Includes selected tips on hold'em, 7-card stud, draw, lowball, tournaments, more. 160 pages, $12.95.

HOLD'EM WISDOM FOR ALL PLAYERS by Daniel Negreanu. Superstar poker player Daniel Negreanu provides 50 easy-to-read and right-to-the-point hold'em strategy nuggets that will immediately make you a better player at cash games and tournaments. His wit and wisdom makes for great reading; even better, it makes for killer winning advice. Conversational, straightforward, and educational, this book covers topics as diverse as the top 10 rookie mistakes to bullying bullies and exploiting your table image.176 pages, paperback, $14.95.

MILLION DOLLAR HOLD'EM: Limit Cash Games by Johnny Chan & Mark Karowe. Learn how to win money at limit hold'em, poker's most popular cash game. You'll get a rare opportunity to get into the mind of the man who has won 10 World Series titles—tied for the most with Doyle Brunson—as the authors pick out illustrative hands and show how they think their way through the bets and the bluffs. No book so thoroughly details the thought process of how a hand should be played, how it could have been played, and the best way to consistently win. 368 pages, paperback, $29.95.

GREAT CARDOZA POKER BOOKS
ADD THESE TO YOUR LIBRARY - ORDER NOW!

CRASH COURSE IN BEATING TEXAS HOLD'EM *by Avery Cardoza.* Perfect for beginning and somewhat experienced players who want to jump right into the action and play cash games, local tournaments, online poker, and the big televised tournaments where millions of dollars can be made. Both limit and no-limit hold'em games are covered, along with the essential strategies needed to play profitably on the pre-flop, flop, turn, and river. The good news is that you don't need to memorize hands or be burdened by math to be a winner—just play by the no-nonsense basic principles outlined in this book. There's a lot of money to be made and Cardoza shows you how to go and get it. 208 pages, $14.95

WINNER'S GUIDE TO TEXAS HOLD'EM POKER *by Ken Warren.* You'll learn how to play every hand from every position with every type of flop. Learn the 14 categories of starting hands, the 10 most common hold'em tells, how to evaluate a game for profit, the value of deception, the art of bluffing, eight secrets to winning, starting hand categories, position, and more! Includes detailed analysis of the top 40 hands and the most complete chapter on hold'em odds in print. Over 400,000 copies sold! 224 pages, $16.95.

HOW TO PLAY WINNING POKER *by Avery Cardoza.* New and completely updated, this classic has sold more than 250,000 copies. Includes major new coverage on playing and winning tournaments, online poker, limit and no-limit hold'em, Omaha games, seven-card stud, and draw poker (including triple draw). Includes 21 essential winning concepts of poker, 15 concepts of bluffing, how to use psychology and body language to get an extra edge, plus information on playing online poker. 256 pages, $14.95.

KEN WARREN TEACHES TEXAS HOLD'EM *by Ken Warren.* This is a step-by-step comprehensive manual for making money at hold'em poker. 42 powerful chapters teach you one lesson at a time. Great practical advice and concepts with examples from actual games and how to apply them to your own play. Lessons include: starting cards, playing position, raising, check-raising, tells, game/seat selection, dominated hands, odds, and much more. This book is already a huge fan favorite and best-seller! 416 pages, $26.95.

OMAHA HIGH-LOW: Play to Win with the Odds *by Bill Boston.* Selecting the right hands to play is the most important decision you'll make in Omaha high-low. More than any other poker game, Omaha is driven by hand value. This is the *only* book that shows you the chances that every one of the 5,278 Omaha high-low hands has of winning the high end of the pot, the low end of it, and how often it is expected to scoop all the chips. You get all the vital tools needed to make critical preflop decisions based on the results of more than 500 million computerized hand simulations. You'll learn the 100 most profitable Omaha high-low starting cards, trap hands to avoid, 49 worst hands, 30 ace-less hands that can be played for profit, and the three bandit cards you must know to avoid unnecessarily losing hands. 248 pages, $19.95.

POKER TALK: Learn How to Talk Poker Like a Pro *by Avery Cardoza.* This fascinating and fabulous collection of colorful poker words, phrases, and poker-speak features more than 2,000 definitions. No longer is it enough to know how to walk the walk in poker, you need to know how to talk the talk! Learn what it means to go all in on a rainbow flop with pocket rockets and get it cracked by cowboys, put a bad beat on a calling station, and go over the top of a producer fishing for a gutshot to win a big dime. You'll soon have those railbirds wondering what *you* are talking about. 304 pages, $9.95.

HOW TO WIN AT OMAHA HIGH-LOW POKER *by Mike Cappelletti.* Clearly written strategies and powerful advice shows the essential winning strategies for beating Omaha high-low poker! This money-making guide includes more than 60 hard-hitting sections on Omaha. Players learn the rules of play, best starting hands, strategies for the flop, turn, and river, how to read the board for both high and low, dangerous draws, and how to beat low-limit tournaments. Includes odds charts, glossary and low-limit tips. 304 pgs, $19.95.

THE CHAMPIONSHIP SERIES
POWERFUL BOOKS YOU <u>MUST</u> HAVE

CHAMPIONSHIP HOLD'EM TOURNAMENT HANDS by *T. J. Cloutier & Tom McEvoy.* An absolute must for hold'em tournament players. Two legends show you how to become a winning tournament player at both limit and no-limit hold'em games. Get inside their heads as they think their way through the correct strategy at 57 limit and no-limit starting hands. Cloutier and McEvoy show you how to use skill and intuition to play strategic hands for maximum profit in real tournament scenarios and how 45 key hands were played by champions in turnaround situations at the WSOP. Gain tremendous insights into how tournament poker is played at the highest levels. 368 pages, $29.95.

CHAMPIONSHIP WIN YOUR WAY INTO BIG MONEY HOLD'EM TOURNAMENTS by *Brad Dougherty & Tom McEvoy.* Every year satellite players win their way into the $10,000 WSOP buy-in event and emerge as millionaires or champions. You can too! Learn from two world champions, the specific, proven strategies for winning almost any satellite. Covers the 10 ways to win a seat at the WSOP, how to win limit hold'em and no-limit hold'em satellites, one-table satellites, online satellites, and the final table of super satellites. Includes a special chapter on no-limit hold'em satellites! 320 pages, $29.95.

CHAMPIONSHIP TOURNAMENT POKER by *Tom McEvoy.* Enthusiastically endorsed by more than five world champions, this is a *must* for every player's library. McEvoy lets you in on the secrets he has used to win millions of dollars in tournaments and the insights he has learned competing against the best players in the world. Packed solid with winning strategies for 11 games with extensive discussions of 7-card stud, limit hold'em, pot and no-limit hold'em, Omaha high-low, re-buy, half-and-half tournaments, satellites, and includes strategies for each stage of tournaments. 416 pages, $29.95.

HOW TO WIN NO-LIMIT HOLD'EM TOURNAMENTS by *Tom McEvoy & Don Vines.* Learn the basic concepts of tournament strategy and how to win big by playing small buy-in events, graduate to medium and big buy-in tournaments, adjust for short fields, huge fields, and slow and fast-action events. Plus how to win online no-limit tournaments. You'll also learn how to manage a tournament bankroll and get tips on table demeanor for televised tournaments. See actual hands played by finalists at WSOP and WPT championship tables with card pictures, analysis and useful lessons from the play. 376 pages, $29.95.

POKER TOURNAMENT TIPS FROM THE PROS by *Shane Smith.* Essential advice from poker theorists, authors, and tournament winners on the best strategies for winning the big prizes at low-limit rebuy tournaments. Learn the best strategies for each of the four stages of play—opening, middle, late and final—how to avoid 26 potential traps, advice on rebuys, aggressive play, clock-watching, inside moves, top 20 tips for winning tournaments, and more. Advice from McEvoy, Caro, Malmuth, Ciaffone, others. 160 pages, $19.95.

NO-LIMIT TEXAS HOLD'EM: The New Player's Guide to Winning Poker's Biggest Game by *Brad Daugherty & Tom McEvoy.* For experienced limit players who want to play no-limit or rookies who have never played before, two world champions give readers a crash course in how to join the elite ranks of million-dollar, no-limit hold'em tournament winners and cash game players. You'll learn the four essential winning skills: how to evaluate the strength of a hand, how to determine the amount to bet, how to understand opponents' play, and how to bluff and when to do it. 74 game scenarios and two unique betting charts for tournament play and sections on essential principles and strategies, show you how to get to the winners circle. Special section on beating online tournaments. 288 pages, $24.95.

CARDOZA POKER BOOKS
POWERFUL INFORMATION YOU MUST HAVE

CHAMPIONSHIP NO-LIMIT & POT-LIMIT HOLD'EM *by T. J. Cloutier & Tom McEvoy*. This is the bible of winning pot-limit and no-limit hold'em tournaments. You'll get all the answers here—no holds barred—to your most important questions: How do you get inside your opponents' heads and learn how to beat them at their own game? How can you tell how much to bet, raise, and reraise in no-limit hold'em? When can you bluff? How do you set up your opponents in pot-limit hold'em so that you can win a monster pot? What are the best strategies for winning no-limit and pot-limit tournaments, satellites, and supersatellites? Rock-solid and inspired advice you can bank on from two of the most recognizable figures in poker. 304 pages, $29.95.

CHAMPIONSHIP HOLD'EM *by T. J. Cloutier & Tom McEvoy*. Hard-hitting hold'em the way it's played *today* in both limit cash games and tournaments. Get killer advice on how to win more money in rammin'-jammin' games, kill-pot, jackpot, shorthanded, and full table cash games. You'll learn the thinking process before the flop, and on the flop, turn, and river with specific suggestions for what to do when good or bad things happen. Plus 20 illustrated hands with play-by-play analyses, specific advice for rocks in tight games, weaklings in loose games, experts in solid games, how hand values change in jackpot games, when you should fold, check, raise, reraise, check-raise, slowplay, and bluff. Also tournament strategies for small buy-in, big buy-in, rebuy, add-on, satellite and big-field major tournaments. Wow! If you want to win at limit hold'em, you need this book! 392 pages, $29.95.

CHAMPIONSHIP OMAHA (Omaha High-Low, Pot-limit Omaha, Limit High Omaha) *by Tom McEvoy & T. J. Cloutier*. Clearly-written strategies and powerful advice from Cloutier and McEvoy who have won four World Series of Poker Omaha titles. Powerful advice shows you how to win at low-limit and high-stakes games, how to play against loose and tight opponents, and the differing strategies for rebuy and freezeout tournaments. Learn the best starting hands, when slowplaying a big hand is dangerous, what danglers are and why winners don't play them, why pot-limit Omaha is the only poker game where you sometimes fold the nuts on the flop and are correct in doing so, and, overall, how you can win a lot of money at Omaha! 296 pages, illustrations, $29.95.

CHAMPIONSHIP TABLE (at the World Series of Poker) *by Dana Smith, Ralph Wheeler, & Tom McEvoy*. *Championship Table* celebrates three decades of poker greats who have competed to win poker's most coveted title. This book gives you the names and photographs of all the players who made the final table, pictures the last hand the champion played against the runner-up, how they played their cards, how much they won, plus fascinating interviews and conversations with the champions. This fascinating and invaluable resource book includes tons of vintage photographs. 208 pages, $19.95.

HOW TO WIN THE CHAMPIONSHIP: Hold'em Strategies for the Final Table, *by T. J. Cloutier*. If you're hungry to win a championship, this is the book that will pave the way to success! T. J. Cloutier, the greatest tournament poker player ever—he has won 59 major tournament titles and appeared at 39 final tables at the WSOP, both more than any other player in the history of poker—shows how to get to the final table where the big money is made and then how to win it all. You'll learn how to build up enough chips to make it through the early and middle rounds and then how to employ T. J.'s own strategies to outmaneuver opponents at the final table and win championships. T. J. shows you how to adjust your play depending upon stack sizes, antes and blinds, table position, opponents' styles, and chip counts. You'll also learn the specific strategies needed for full tables and for six-handed, three-handed, and heads-up play. 288 pages, $29.95.

POWERFUL POKER SIMULATIONS
A MUST FOR SERIOUS PLAYERS WITH A COMPUTER!
IBM compatible CD ROM Win 95, 98, 2000, NT, ME, XP

These incredible full color poker simulations are the best method to improve your game. Computer opponents play like real players. All games let you set the limits and rake and have fully programmable players, plus stat tracking, and Hand Analyzer for starting hands. MIke Caro, the world's foremost poker theoretician says, "Amazing... a steal for under $500... get it, it's great." Includes free phone support. "Smart Advisor" gives expert advice for every play!

1. TURBO TEXAS HOLD'EM FOR WINDOWS - $59.95. Choose which players, and how many (2-10) you want to play, create loose/tight games, and control check-raising, bluffing, position, sensitivity to pot odds, and more! Also, instant replay, pop-up odds, Professional Advisor keeps track of play statistics. Free bonus: Hold'em Hand Analyzer analyzes all 169 pocket hands in detail and their win rates under any conditions you set. Caro says this "hold'em software is the most powerful ever created." Great product!

2. TURBO SEVEN-CARD STUD FOR WINDOWS - $59.95. Create any conditions of play; choose number of players (2-8), bet amounts, fixed or spread limit, bring-in method, tight/loose conditions, position, reaction to board, number of dead cards, and stack deck to create special conditions. Features instant replay. Terrific stat reporting includes analysis of starting cards, 3-D bar charts, and graphs. Play interactively and run high speed simulation to test strategies. Hand Analyzer analyzes starting hands in detail. Wow!

3. TURBO OMAHA HIGH-LOW SPLIT FOR WINDOWS - $59.95. Specify any playing conditions, including betting limits, number of raises, blind structures, button position, aggressiveness/passiveness of opponents, number of players (2-10), types of hands dealt, blinds, position, board reaction, and specify flop, turn, and river cards! Choose opponents and use provided point count or create your own. Statistical reporting, instant replay, pop-up odds high speed simulation to test strategies, amazing Hand Analyzer, and much more!

4. TURBO OMAHA HIGH FOR WINDOWS - $59.95. Same features as above, but tailored for Omaha High only. Caro says program is "an electrifying research tool...it can clearly be worth thousands of dollars to any serious player. A must for Omaha High players."

5. TURBO 7 STUD 8 OR BETTER - $59.95. Brand new with all the features you expect from the Wilson Turbo products: the latest artificial intelligence, instant advice and exact odds, play versus 2-7 opponents, enhanced data charts that can be exported or printed, the ability to fold out of turn and immediately go to the next hand, ability to peek at opponent's hand, optional warning mode that warns you if a play disagrees with the advisor, and automatic mode that runs up to 50 tests unattended. Tough computer players vary their styles for a great game.

6. TOURNAMENT TEXAS HOLD'EM - $39.95
Set-up for tournament practice and play, this realistic simulation pits you against celebrity look-alikes. Tons of options let you control tournament size with 10 to 300 entrants, select limits, ante, rake, blind structures, freezeouts, number of rebuys, and competition level of opponents. Pop-up status report shows how you're doing vs. the competition. Save tournaments in progress to play again later. Additional feature allows quick folds on finished hands.

Order now at 1-800-577-WINS or go online to:www.cardozapub.com